A Short Guide to Writing about Music

THE SHORT GUIDE SERIES

Under the Editorship of
SYLVAN BARNET
MARCIA STUBBS

A Short Guide to Writing about Music

SECOND EDITION

JONATHAN D. BELLMAN
University of Northern Colorado

PEARSON
Longman

New York   San Francisco   Boston
London   Toronto   Sydney   Tokyo   Singapore   Madrid
Mexico City   Munich   Paris   Cape Town   Hong Kong   Montreal

Publisher: Joseph Opiela
Marketing Manager: Thomas DeMarco
Production Manager: Savoula Amanatidis
Project Coordination, Text Design, and Electronic Page Makeup: GGS Book Services
Cover Designer/Manager: John Callahan
Cover Illustration/Photo: Getty Images, Inc.
Manufacturing Manager: Mary Fischer
Printer and Binder: R. R. Donnelley & Sons Company—Harrisonburg
Cover Printer: The Lehigh Press, Inc.

Library of Congress Cataloging-in-Publication Data

Bellman, Jonathan D.
    A short guide to writing about music / Jonathan D. Bellman.—2nd ed.
        p. cm.— (The short guide series)
    Includes index.
    ISBN 0-321-18791-1 (paperback)
        1. Music—Historiography—Handbooks, manuals, etc.   2. Musical
criticism—Authorship—Handbooks, manuals, etc.   I. Title.   II. Series.

ML3797.B4 2006
808'.06678—dc22

                                                    2005058681

Please visit our website at *http://www.ablongman.com*

ISBN 0-321-18791-1

1 2 3 4 5 6 7 8 9 10—DOH—09 08 07 06

For my parents:

Samuel Irving Bellman
(*Professor Emeritus of English, California State Polytechnic University, Pomona*), *who devoted much of his professional life to teaching writing to the undergraduates of the state of California;*

Jeanne Lisker Bellman,
who taught her sons;

and my wife and son:

Deborah Ann Kauffman and Benjamin Howard Bellman—
mihi vita cariores sunt.

Contents

Preface

People who devote their lives to music are a passionate and quixotic lot, from the primary school music teacher to international concert artist, from local concert reviewer to professional scholar and researcher. Writing about music demands the same wild-eyed commitment that we give to teaching, playing, and studying it, but it also requires the same dogged practice to ensure that the end product reflects balance and control. *That* involves something very different from passionate, quixotic, wild-eyed commitment. I seek to provide some guidance both for freeing and controlling the inner writer.

After an introductory chapter, *A Short Guide to Writing about Music*, Second Edition, is for the most part organized by task, such as writing reviews, analyses, essays, research papers, and preparing a final manuscript. Because the different genres of writing about music have different requirements and protocols, this seemed to be the most pragmatic way of going about it; readers would know exactly where to go. Chapter 1 (and perhaps Chapter 2, depending on the reader's background) should probably be read first, therefore, and the following chapters should be read in an order reflecting the reader's needs. But there is a good deal of cross-applicability: Chapter 8, "Style in Writing," is relevant to all writers, as are the instructions regarding musical examples in Chapter 9, the section "Hints on Beginning" in Chapter 5, and so on. Probably the best way to begin to use this book is to skim the whole of it before proceeding in more detail.

I do not intend this book to supersede such works as *The Elements of Style*, Fourth Edition, by William Strunk, Jr., and E. B. White, *Writing about Music* by D. Kern Holoman, or *A Manual for Writers of Term Papers, Theses, and Dissertations*, Sixth Edition, by Kate L. Turabian. Strunk and White's pithy work ought to be read regularly by all English-language writers, and the style manuals by Holoman and Turabian go into far more detail regarding various guidelines than I am able to do here. I have both drawn guidance and occasionally departed from these works, all of which are invaluable to serious writers.

ACKNOWLEDGMENTS

Permissions for quoted material were graciously provided by Oxford University Press, the University of California Press, the University Press of New England, Taylor & Francis publishers, Musica Rara publications, and *Stereo Review/High Fidelity*. I am especially grateful to Robert Matheu of *CREEM* magazine and John Morthland, co-executor of the Lester Bangs estate, for the permission to use Bangs's words, and to NME for permission to use the words of Nick Kent. Thanks also to Alfred Publishing for permission to use the excerpts from the music of George Gershwin. Students and friends whose writing appears here include Jeff Simpson, Amie Margoles, Jessica Mosier, Matthew Larson, Dawn Kummer, Susan Nelson, Professor Alejandro E. Planchart, Professor James Parakilas, Professor Scott Warfield, and the late Professor Steven Gilbert. I am grateful to you all. I am also indebted to those who advised, read, explained, and provided myriad other kinds of help: Professor Deborah Kauffman (of course!), Professor Stephen A. Luttmann, Professor Marian Wilson Kimber, Professor John Michael Cooper, Lyle Neff, Pietro Moretti, and probably others whose forgiveness I humbly beg. Finally, to Professor Thomas Mathiesen, a deep bow of gratitude for a certain beautiful and apposite Latin phrase. The joy I take in being part of such a flourishing and supportive musical, cultural, academic, and scholarly community cannot be overstated.

JONATHAN D. BELLMAN
Greeley, CO
February 2006

1

WRITING ABOUT MUSIC

There is so much talk about music and so little is said. I believe that words are not at all up to it, and if I should find that they were adequate I would stop making music altogether.[1]

—FELIX MENDELSSOHN

WORDS ABOUT MUSIC: WHY?

Most musicians can sympathize with the composer Robert Schumann's famous musing, "But why so many words about music? The best discourse on music is silence. . . . Away with your musical journals!" Even acknowledging the irony of Schumann's comment—he helped found a music journal and served as its chief editor for roughly eleven years—many would agree that there seems to be something odd, almost wasteful, about the number of words written about music, an art needing no words to exist. Another nineteenth-century figure, the essayist and critic Walter Pater, apparently agreed: "All art," he wrote, "constantly aspires to the condition of music," and it is tempting to conclude that prose treatments of music are therefore superfluous. What already resides on Mt. Olympus, so to speak, has no need of wings to get there.

If, as Pater implies, the other arts seek to achieve what music already has, students may find the comments of Mendelssohn and Schumann attractive. If there is little point to writing about music, after all, then there

---

[1]Mendelssohn, letter of 15 October 1842, quoted in *Source Readings in Music History* (1950), ed. Oliver Strunk, vol. 6 (rev. ed.), *The Nineteenth Century*, ed. Ruth Solie (New York: W. W. Norton, 1998), 159.

is less point in reading about how to write about it. But—before you gleefully shut this book—are we sure what Pater meant? Does he suggest that all art seeks to be lovely, or to produce certain emotions within the listener's soul? That all art seeks to function as light entertainment, to allow us at least a vague pleasure when our full attention is not focused, or to motivate us to a particular behavior, such as dancing or sleeping? Certainly, different kinds of music can do all these things. Or, rather, did Pater mean that the other arts envy music's capacity for direct-to-the-heart communication, its freedom from words and representative images?

The questions raised by Pater's seemingly clear assertion illustrate the need for writing about music. They also indicate why it is such a tricky business. A constant in civilization since ancient times, music has always been notoriously hard to describe; such questions as how it "works," what effect it has on listeners, and what point it seeks to make are frequently asked but never fully answered. In a sense, then, there is never enough writing about music. Every writer has, potentially, something to contribute.

Just what this contribution is may not be apparent at first. In my experience as a writer and teacher, worthwhile ideas result most often from insistent questioning of and dogged reflection upon the subject. The questioning should happen before the writing begins in earnest and as the early drafts develop. I do not mean to suggest that the idea-generating process stops when the writing begins; further ideas will certainly evolve throughout the writing process. Before pen meets paper, though, or fingers meet keyboard, the author must have *some* idea of the points that need to be made. Since writing is the process that will ultimately fashion ideas, once they exist, into clear and coherent form, the real work can only begin once they are in place.

The author's primary obligation is twofold. First, ideas must be expressed with a certain degree of confidence. The author must believe in them, certain that he or she is not merely parroting clichés or casually acquired thoughts too new or unexamined to defend. Second, the author must distrust what at the moment seem to be good ideas and be willing to go through a painful evaluation process, revising draft after draft in an effort to refine the idea and perfect the mode of expression. Writing is both art and craft, and it requires as much work as does music-making itself—perfecting one's instrumental or vocal expertise or developing a personal compositional language. The initial draft, the first exposition of ideas, is only the beginning.

This may seem daunting. How can one be confident of his or her ideas and writing, yet still know when to be dissatisfied with a draft? How can one go about expressing opinions and summarizing research when the intended audience (a professor, say) has a good deal more experience and training? How can one even *begin*, given the risks?

Answer: start somewhere. Start where you are right now.

CHOOSING AN AUDIENCE

Judging from the remark quoted at the beginning of this chapter, Mendelssohn might well have agreed with an even more blunt observation: a good deal of writing on musical subjects fails utterly. This failure has less to do with the use of advanced musical vocabulary, a common complaint, than with the neglect of two key questions that must be answered before writing begins. They are: For whom am I writing? and How can I best reach this audience? These seemingly obvious questions require careful consideration. The answers will ultimately dictate the amount of technical terminology, the level of prose, the length of the analytical discussions, and the balance you strike between musical and non-musical material (historical background, for example).

For example, the opening phrase "Beethoven, German-born and reared in the Classical tradition" would probably be inappropriate for a music major's music history paper because that information is common knowledge among musicians. On the other hand, newspaper readers or a concert audience might find this information helpful, because it turns a name into a human being. Conversely, if in writing about Beethoven's Op. 53 piano sonata ("Waldstein") one comments on how interesting it is that the second theme of the first movement is introduced in the mediant rather than the dominant key, only trained musicians will have any idea what is being discussed.

Writing too ambitiously for either the reader's or one's own level of experience can be even more inappropriate. For example, a sentence that begins "Since Beethoven was a titan who spanned Classic and Romantic eras" will be meaningless to virtually everyone, even though it is the sort of bromide often encountered in music appreciation texts and recording liner notes. Novice readers with no knowledge of style periods will not understand what such a sentence means, and those with more musical experience will know that it is by no means the obvious fact it seems to be. Such a statement cannot be made without addressing the extent to which Beethoven was Classic or Romantic, the ways in which he might be considered a "titan," and so on. One of the most basic rules of writing is that an author never make statements he or she is not prepared to defend.

We will return to these issues as we discuss specific types of writing. Let it suffice here to say that successful writing about music amounts to far more than the correct use of terminology. If an author is to be read and understood, careful consideration of the audience's level of understanding is crucially important in choosing content and developing an appropriate writing style.

KINDS OF WRITING

Only a portion of "writing about music" consists of discussion of the music itself. Other components may include biographical and historical background, discussions of instruments, considerations of the ways music is understood in society, and inquiries into music's relationship to the other arts and to the wider culture. An essay, paper, column, or book about music may approach the subject from an analytical standpoint (examining just how musical works operate), or it may address performance matters, cultural contexts, the physical source material for the music, or any number of other perspectives. Above all, writers must be aware of the variety of tools available.

Here are some common approaches to writing about music.

History and Biography

History and biography are genres of writing that examine the circumstances and people that produced a work or a repertory, situating works in the musical and cultural environments of their time. This information, relevant in some measure to almost any kind of writing about music, is particularly valued among the general readership. Many people are fascinated by the musical life, and feel a kind of deeper personal connection with their favorite musicians; biographical treatments offer these readers additional personal, musical, or psychological insight into the composers and performers of the music they love. Its appeal is such that, for many, biography is their first (and possibly only) venture beyond listening.

Historical and biographical treatments of musical subjects can overlap a good deal. History is made up of the doings of people, after all, and individuals cannot properly be studied in the absence of historical context. In an introductory note, after telling us that "this book is not a biography in the ordinary sense," the author of a famous example of such a blend comments,

> In the battle of Berlioz with his age a typical story is dramatized by the events themselves. History spins the plot around the Artist, and the four corners of our society are illumined like a stage. For in a high civilization all social facts and forces become the matrix, and sometimes the subject, of the artist's work; and in the forms and conditions of a collective art like music we find again the elements of familiar history— politics, economics, and the struggles of human groups.[2]

Individuals can even disappear into the historical fog for lack of records. A study of Florentine Renaissance carnival songs, for example, will of necessity dwell not on the composers but on the songs themselves and their carnival circumstances because substantial information on the majority of the composers is lost. But when biographical information is available, it will often be an important element of a historical study. Biographical and historical studies can be among the most easy to read and assimilate, and they speak to the entire musically inclined readership.

Style Study

Style studies take as their point of departure music's raw materials: its melodies, harmonies, meters and rhythms, scoring, and other basic ingredients. How these core elements become a "style" suitable for examination is better illustrated by example than by description, so let us glance at the American children's folk song, "Go Tell Aunt Rhody" (shown in Example 1.1).

The text is mock-solemn, gravely acknowledging a death. Death in the adult world would occasion mourning, and indeed later verses have the gander and goslings weeping. That this is really a children's joke, however, is shown by the line, "she died in the mill-pond, standing on her head." The music, known to children all over the United States from folk and school settings, complements the text in several ways.

[2]Jacques Barzun, *Berlioz and the Romantic Century*, 2 vols. (Boston: Little, Brown, 1950), I, [xvi].

Go Tell Aunt Rhody

American Folk Song

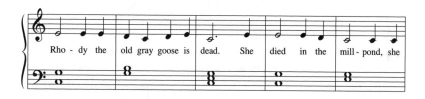

EX. 1.1

American children's folk song, "Go Tell Aunt Rhody."

That is, the musical *materials* are completely appropriate to the words and to the message they convey.

The melody consists only of the first five notes of a major scale—playable on the piano without moving one's hand, singable by an untrained child's voice—and thus evokes children's music-making. The rhythmic vocabulary is simple, without syncopations or rhythmic complexities, and motion is based on an even quarter-note pulse with short, regular phrases. There are only two chords, tonic and dominant, so the harmonic language is limited to the chord that gives the greatest sense of rest and repose (the tonic) and the chord that most wants to go to it (the dominant). There is more, but the point is made: the musical language of this song, the composite sound produced by its materials, perfectly suits the words. The text bespeaks childlike simplicity, and the music is composed of the most basic materials available. The *style* of this song, in other words, perfectly suits its text.

Style studies often include actual or implied comparison, which is necessary in order to answer a variety of questions. The goals of such studies vary, perhaps involving the identification of the composer (when his or her identity is in doubt) or the dating of a work (as when the style of a piece is found to be more typical of a composer's earlier rather than later writing). Style studies can also address national style or influence, or cast light on a composer's musical sources. The basis of style inquiry is musical materials: what a piece of music is made of, and what makes its sound a distinctive one.

One natural outgrowth of style study consists of investigations into what particular styles meant to their original audiences. The musical language chosen by a composer often holds meanings for its contemporary audience that are lost to later generations of listeners. Jazz provides a good example: what is now a popular and honored American idiom originally had connotations of decadence, sexuality, even danger. These disreputable associations became particularly significant when the jazz language was used in concert works; the use of what was perceived as a low-class, forbidden music in an elevated concert context had a powerful effect on audiences of the 1920s and 1930s. Today's average concertgoer, happy to hear frequent performances of popular Gershwin and Ravel works, probably has little idea of how such music was originally heard. A style study on this topic might point out both what elements are jazz-derived ("blue notes," for example, and certain dance rhythms) and how the music was understood, thus addressing both materials and significance.

Analysis

Analysis consists of coming to an understanding of the structure and processes of a piece, or "how it works." It differs from style study in that it primarily investigates how the notes of a piece relate to each other rather than to a widely understood musical language or to extramusical ideas. Analysts proceed from a variety of approaches, including harmonic (or vertical), melodic (or linear), textural, and rhythmic. It is impossible to analyze music (or to understand another's analysis) without full musical literacy and a command of technical vocabulary. Accordingly, analyses usually make the toughest reading, not only because of the density of the subject matter, but also because of the necessity for frequent reference to score examples. The best analyses are written by those with a good deal of experience with music study. Chapter 3 addresses the challenges of writing musical analysis.

Performance Study

Discussions of the way music works in performance are central to writing on musical subjects. Concert reviews focus on this aspect, but any musical writing gains substantially by viewing music within a performance context. All aspects of performance are relevant: how music unfolds in real time and the physical aspects of sound production; how well the performer(s) did; how coherent and effective a piece is as performed (as opposed to its potential on paper); how it makes the listener feel; and its overall effect. Performance studies address music as realized, how it is heard and understood, rather than consider it simply as text.

A subcategory of performance studies is *Performance Practices*, which investigates the historical context of musical performance. The underlying assumption of this discipline is that consideration of historical performance circumstances is necessary for a solid understanding of any music, including the most familiar masterworks. Among the elements of historical performance are period instruments and how they sounded (as closely as we can approximate them); techniques and methods of playing the instruments; how much and what kinds of ornamentation need to be supplied by the performer; the size and seating (or standing) arrangement of ensembles; performance etiquette for musicians and audience alike; performance spaces and their acoustics; and the ways in which musical notations, both archaic and current, have been understood and realized in performance.

Organological, Archival, and Source Studies

Organological, archival, and source studies are usually written by and for research specialists. Organology is the study of musical instruments; *organological studies* are often technical, primarily concerned with physical aspects and questions of instrumental development. *Archival studies* address music at least several centuries old and surviving principally in manuscripts; they are so called because the music and related materials (e.g., pay receipts, court and church records, baptismal certificates, death notices) survive principally in archives. *Source studies* examine such musical documents as compositional sketches and variant manuscripts and editions. Such studies are not limited to early music, but they share with archival studies the necessity of painstaking examination of primary sources, including identifications of paper type, ink composition, and handwriting. Like archival studies, the attention to such details serves broader musical and historical goals, such as a better understanding of a composer's compositional process or a clear picture of the dissemination patterns of a particular repertory.

CRITICISM

Music criticism consists of explanation and evaluation of works or performances, which, like analysis, may be accomplished in a variety of ways. All critical writing is based on informed opinion; one (presumably authoritative) author's view is intended to inform and illuminate many readers. The idea of "informed opinion" can, however, be confusing. Embedded in this common phrase are two discrete but overlapping concepts: *opinions* and *values*. We want and expect opinions from critics but have a right to expect more than "Wagner's music is an affront to taste" or "modern concert music is raucous and incoherent." These two simple statements of preference approach a chocolate-vs.-vanilla level of subjectivity, for which reason they may not profitably be disputed. They might seem authoritative, but they are not.

Every critic proceeds from personal values (that is, principles or standards) that—ideally—represent more than mere preferences, that presumably were adopted after some consideration, and that may be expected to stand up to scrutiny and debate. These values might include "live performance is integral to musical art," "the study of historical performance traditions and techniques leads to better understanding of the music," or "support of music by living composers keeps the concert tradition vital." Advocates of recordings-*as*-performance might challenge the first example, partisans of traditional conservatory education might dispute the second, and many contemporary listeners would dispute the third, but they are principled positions that may be defended with logic, argument, and example. They are not mere statements of taste. (But compare these dissenting positions with, for example, "Wagner is great" or "modern concert music is *not* raucous and incoherent," which are still no more than opinions.) Plausible objections help establish ideas as *values*—philosophical stances—that will inform critical evaluations and support or refute other critical opinions. This emphasis on both the principles that guide critical judgment and the *reasoning* that proceeds from them distinguishes them from mere opinions.

One common type of criticism is the concert review. This staple of music journalism, generally intended for a wide readership, seeks to evaluate what took place at a particular event, both to offer an assessment for the benefit of those who were not able to attend and to provide another perspective for those who did—not only describing what was played and how well, but offering commentary reflecting the reviewer's values and beliefs. (For more discussion of the reviewing process, see Chapter 2.) A related journalistic genre, although one requiring more experience, is program and liner notes, which normally provide brief discussions of works to be performed in concert or included on a recording. Here, explanation is far more important than evaluation; the goal is to enhance the listening experience for a broad range of listeners. (For more on this kind of writing, see Chapter 4.)

More specialized music criticism often examines the music in terms of beauty, effectiveness, or artistic merit. One of the most common techniques is comparison: works of the same or similar genres, or historical periods, or composers, may be examined in light of each other. A clearer picture of a work is thus achieved by viewing it in a broader musical environment.

Still another type of criticism examines music in the light of culture and society, past and present. A critique of this kind takes as its departure point the idea that musical works do not appear in a vacuum; they reflect, in key ways, the perspectives of the society and composer that produce them. As later listeners probably have radically different perspectives and experience, such commentaries on the hearing, perception, and "meaning" of music seek to place it in a multiplicity of contexts and to examine its significance outside the concert hall and classroom. There are several common approaches to this kind of criticism.

Marxist Criticism

Drawing on the polarized economic and political models of Marxist thought (have vs. have-not, privileged vs. oppressed, majority vs. minority, capitalist vs. worker, and so on), Marxist criticism has provided the starting point for many critical schools. Critique in this sense is almost always a challenge; the critical perspective is one of resistance or interrogation, seeking to expose the assumptions inherent in a musical work, repertory, or school. The point is not the identification of works that meet appropriate criteria or sufficiently challenge the majority viewpoint or artistic status quo, but rather the enlightenment that results from the dialogue between work (or popular taste) and criticism.

Here is an excerpt by Theodor Adorno, a central figure in Marxist musical criticism and one of the thinkers most cited by later critical schools:

> Music is ideological where the circumstances of production in it gain primacy over the productive forces. What should be shown is what can make it ideological: engendering a false consciousness; transfiguring so as to divert from the banality of existence; duplicating and thus only re-inforcing that existence; and above all, abstract affirmation. One may postulate that intramusical ideologies are recognizable by immanent discord in the works. . . . But diagnosis and analysis of ideologies do not exhaust the music-sociological interest in them. The same attention should be paid to the ways in which ideologies prevail in practical musi-cal life, i.e., to the ideologies *about* music. Today ideology is apt to be entangled with violent naiveté. Music is unthinkingly accepted as a proffered consumer commodity, like the cultural sphere as a whole; it is affirmed because it is there, without much reference to its concrete nature.[3]

The most common Marxist preoccupations, here associated with music, are all present: identification of operative baleful ideologies; ide-ologies that remain unquestioned by those most susceptible to them; a pitiless market producing manipulative entertainment products that reinforce abstract affirmation and divert attention from the "banality of existence"; reinforcement of the unjust economic model (music being "unthinkingly accepted as a proffered consumer commodity"); and so on. This adversarial model is to be found in virtually all the critical schools.

Soviet Pseudo-Marxist Criticism

A critical stance purporting to be Marxian was common (indeed, state sponsored and required) in Soviet countries before the fall of the Berlin Wall, and such criticism is still commonly found on library shelves. One

---

[3]Theodor W. Adorno, *Introduction to the Sociology of Music* [1962], trans. E. B. Ashton (New York: Seabury Press, 1976), 223–24.

of the hallmarks of such criticism is that it seems to be applied in a somewhat chaotic and often heavy-handed way, as when a sudden political interpretation intrudes in an otherwise nonpolitical discussion. This is one
indication of the influence of government censors and ideologues, rather
than the opinion of the music critic him- or herself. The following passage is about an old Hungarian folksong of the question-and-answer type
in which an elderly villager gives directions to his master (text: "Gaffer,
gaffer, which is the way to Becskerek? Master, master, this is the way
to Becskerek"). The ideological intrusions seem, to my eye at least,
unnecessary:

> This simple, popular melody, or fragment of a melody, consisting of
> four notes . . . represents the earliest written record of Hungarian
> music. It is on the boundary of the old and the new period and with it
> begins the history of Hungarian music recorded in musical notation. It
> would seem that the "peasant voice" inherent in this music often
> "showed the way" when the culture of the rulers had a tendency to go
> astray, and it was a strange reminder at a time when the suppression of
> the peasant revolts and the petrification of the feudal society, amid the
> increasing exactions of Vienna and Constantinople[,] bore the country
> the catastrophe of Mohács, and centuries of crises.[4]

Bence Szabolcsi, the author, seems most interested in the early history of Hungarian written music, and the process by which folk music
evolved and broadened into popular and cultivated music. This passage is
from Szabolcsi's *Concise History of Hungarian Music*, and in that kind of
a general work the gratuitous comments on "the culture of the rulers"
and the way that the "peasant voice . . . showed the way" seem not only
beside the point but also faintly ridiculous.

Cultural Criticism

Criticism from the perspective of social or cultural history examines the
way music relates to its cultural surroundings, whether these surroundings are from its own time or the present. Susan McClary encapsulated

---

[4]Bence Szabolcsi, *A Concise History of Hungarian Music*, trans. Sára Karig (London:
Barrie & Rockliff in cooperation with Corvina Press in Budapest, 1964), 23. Szabolcsi
was for a long time one of the central figures in Hungarian musicology, and particularly because of the publication date I suspect that the inclusion of this passage had
more to do with the Soviet censors than with his own historical view.

the concerns of cultural criticism in her study of a Mozart piano concerto movement, a work which

> neither makes up its own rules nor derives them from some abstract, absolute, transcendental source. Rather it depends heavily on conventions of eighteenth-century harmonic syntax, formal procedure, genre type, rhythmic propriety, gestural vocabulary, and associations. All of these conventions have histories: *social* histories marked with national, economic, class, and gender—that is, political—interests.[5]

Not only the work as a whole, therefore, but every aspect of it is to be considered in the light of the greater culture. So, for example, because rock-and-roll music emerged in the 1950s from various musical styles, it can be studied not only for its musical content but also for the associations listeners had with the musicians who played it—almost exclusively young, often African American, usually rebellious or pretending to be, overtly sexual and *dangerous*—and what such music was thought to convey. Cultural criticism in music often incorporates aspects of style study, history, and biography, which illustrates both that the boundaries separating different types of musical writing are hazy at best, and that different perspectives often inform and supplement one another.

Gender Studies in Music

This area of criticism, encompassing both feminist criticism and gay and lesbian criticism, proceeds from the idea that composers' and listeners' genders and sexual orientations affect not only how music is produced and heard, but also how it is received in society. Despite the focus, gender-based criticism raises a variety of philosophical issues. As Patrice Koelsch suggests,

> One of the original methodologies of feminist criticism is to look for the gaps and listen for the silences. We must learn to see and hear what has been invisible and inaudible to us.[6]

---

[5]Susan McClary, "A Musical Dialectic from the Enlightenment: Mozart's *Piano Concerto in G Major, K. 453*, Movement 2," *Cultural Critique* (Fall 1986), 133–34. Used by permission of Oxford University Press. The italics are in the original.
[6]Patrice Koelsch, "The Criticism of Quality and the Quality of Criticism," *Art Papers* (November–December 1990), 14.

These silences suggest something deeper than the familiar labels "oppressed women" and "marginalized gays." In a study of the seventeenth-century Florentine singer and composer Barbara Strozzi, musicologist Ellen Rosand identifies the differing roles and circumstances of performer and composer, and of female and male musicians, and in doing so seeks to explain why much of the music by women from this period does not survive.

> Although numerous contemporary reports and descriptions bear witness to the existence of highly skilled female singers who graced the courts and theaters of seventeenth-century Italy, we know few compositions by secular women of the period. It is difficult to believe, however, that none of the most celebrated female singers wrote music—at least for their own use. There seems no reason to assume that, in this respect, they would have differed in ability from the ubiquitous, highly esteemed, and famous male singer-composers of the early part of the century. Yet the fact remains that we have very little of their music.
>
> For singers—female as well as male—creating at least some of the music they performed may well have been such an integral aspect of their activity that it was simply taken for granted, viewed as a normal part of the performer's task. If such music has not survived, part of the reason must lie in the fact that it was neither printed nor copied in manuscripts. It may have been partly or totally improvised and thus never committed to paper, even originally. For whatever reason, it was apparently not prized as an object independent of its performance.[7]

A key part of the "listening for the silences" approach has involved the identification of coded cultural meanings (in literature, for example) connecting gay sexuality with musicality and musical practice itself—the old image of music (traceable back to Plato's *Republic*) as an effeminizing pastime for sissies, weaklings, and other "disordered" types. Sophie Fuller and Lloyd Whitesell observe, after discussing some musical euphemisms that refer to gay sexuality in Marcel Proust's novel *Swann in Love*,

> Musical pleasure is a ready figure for the delights of the flesh, a euphemistic figure whose innocent appearance conceals the knowledge of

---

[7]Ellen Rosand, "The Voice of Barbara Strozzi," in *Women Making Music: The Western Art Tradition, 1150–1950*, ed. Jane Bowers and Judith Tick (Urbana and Chicago: University of Illinois Press, 1986), 173.

forbidden practices. For Proust, as for many of his contemporaries, musical expression and the expression of queer sexuality were sympathetically linked. Both depend on mysterious ontogenies of personal preference and innate faculty: "[the inverts'] special taste [is] unconsciously inherited like predispositions for drawing, for music, towards blindness." As the . . . passage implies, both attributes can carry the undertones of an imperfection of character.[8]

Gender studies in music, then, is interested in composers neglected for what some feel are gender-based reasons (Barbara Strozzi, Elizabeth Jacquet de la Guerre, Clara Wieck Schumann, etc.), the gender-related aspects of the lives and music of better known gay composers (Tchaikovsky, Copland, Britten), and composers about whom there continues to be debate (Schubert, Elgar). Beyond that, though, are somewhat subtler, previously neglected questions. Do the different genders and gender orientations tend to compose and perform different kinds of music? Do they hear and interpret music differently? What does music signify for their respective places in society? How does the "gendering" (i.e., associating with or characterizing by a particular gender) of a musical genre affect its subsequent reception? Many of the questions raised by this discipline have sought to broaden the context for music study, reception, and understanding.

All critical approaches are personal and by definition make no claim to objectivity. Gender studies in music is perhaps the most unabashedly personal of all, often blending criticism with open autobiography, even sexual autobiography. While critiquing what is perceived as the "dominant paradigm" in music reception, interpretation, and understanding, this approach also openly celebrates music's sensuality and its relationship to other sensual experiences. It is a specialized area in music criticism, one that continually develops its own vocabulary and approaches, and about which there continues to be a good deal of debate.

Postcolonial Criticism

Postcolonial criticism addresses cultural phenomena such as art, literature, and music from the perspective of the geopolitical and ethnocultural relationships between imperial powers and their subject states and

---

[8]Sophie Fuller and Lloyd Whitesell, Introduction to *Queer Episodes in Music and Modern Identity*, ed. Fuller and Whitesell (Urbana and Chicago: University of Illinois Press, 2002), 2. An "invert" or "sexual invert" is an old clinical term for a gay person.

peoples—in other words, colonizers and colonized. The primary starting
point of this critical stance was Edward Said's book *Orientalism* (1978),
which radically and creatively reinterpreted the word *orientalism* itself.
Orientalism had previously designated a group of linguistic, historical,
and geographical academic disciplines, but Said saw it as the label for
an entire cultural philosophy: the "othering" of the distant cultures
being studied by interpreting them as strange, different, passive, and
feminized—often suspect, in other words, if not openly wrong and cor-
rupt. The often-skewed representation of the Other engendered false
and simplistic representations of distant cultures as both the dominant
culture's most desirable dream and worst nightmare (Islamic culture, for
example, being simultaneously a Disneyland of Arabian Nights-type exotic pleasure, mystery, and allure on the one hand and mindless bar-
barism on the other), and thus made conquest by a dominant power
more palatable in general.

In the following excerpt, John Richardson discusses Philip Glass's
opera *Akhnaten*, which is about an (actual) Egyptian pharaoh who re-
belled against the traditional pantheon and priesthood of Egyptian religion and (for a brief time) established what some consider to be the first
monotheistic religious system. The two issues raised here—pinpointing
characteristics that make music "sound" ancient Egyptian in an exotic
kind of way (whether or not they have anything to do with ancient Egypt
or any other exotic place), and identifying the responsibilities of composer and listener alike to engage and interrogate colonialist assumptions
and stylistic reinscriptions of Self and Other—are central to postcolonial
criticism.

> The crucial question seems to be, therefore, whether there is any-
> thing in the music or the drama that marks the contemporary rather
> than the ancient culture as other and in this way stigmatizes it in the
> eyes or the ears of audiences. . . . There is very little of that kind of
> representation in *Akhnaten*, although there are, admittedly, some mo-
> ments when the music does seem to connote "ancient Egyptianness"
> in a relatively indirect way (in the use of reed and percussion instru-
> ments; in the use of the "lowered" second and third degrees of the
> scale; etc.).
>
> But this does not imply that we should let Glass off the orientalist
> hook altogether; it is possible that *Akhnaten*, like other representations
> of the non-Euro-North American world in recent opera . . . in some
> way "reflects the unequal distribution of power among the nations of

the world."[9] Simply by dint of the massive production and distribution machinery that backs them up, these composers are arguably complicit in some way in the orientalist/capitalist-imperialist project.[10]

The binarisms identified in postcolonial criticism include Self vs. Other, West vs. East, rich country/culture vs. poor country/culture, and tourist vs. native. It offers pointed judgments on the very idea of observation or even the naming of something strange and unfamiliar. It seems fair to say, though, that this perspective is less well developed in the criticism of music than in literary and cultural studies more generally.

THE AUTHOR'S OPINION: CLARITY AND RESTRAINT

In written criticism in particular, and in all writing about music to some extent, there can be no pretense of airtight "proof" or scientific accuracy. The author's opinion can never be fully suppressed, no matter how strenuous the efforts at objectivity may be. This is all to the good; writing is done by human beings, and human beings have values and opinions, register emotional responses, and come to personal conclusions. Decisions regarding which aspects of a musical passage are most salient, what issues should be addressed, and how one should approach a subject all testify to a particular posture and opinion on the part of the author. Complete objectivity is a fiction and should not be pursued as an ideal.

On the other hand, convincing writing on music (or on any subject, for that matter) does not take frequent recourse to unfounded assertions prefaced by "I feel," "it seems to me," "to my mind," and the like. Although these phrases are inherently unobjectionable, you should use them with discretion. Readers have a right to believe that what they are reading is based on more than the author's opinion, even when it is clearly an opinion piece. Those authors who ground their opinions in solid evidence and reasoning—or at least in clearly formulated values—are persuasive, whereas those who merely vent unfounded opinions and gut feelings (in essence, running off at the pen) are wasting the reader's time.

---

[9]Here Richardson quotes Ralph P. Locke, "Constructing the Oriental 'Other': Saint Saëns's *Samson et Dalila*," *Cambridge Opera Journal* 3/3 (1991), 285.
[10]John Richardson, *Singing Archaeology: Philip Glass's* Akhnaten (Hanover, NH and London: Wesleyan University Press, 1999), 195–96.

EX. 1.2
Mozart, Piano Concerto in A Major, K. 488, II, opening.

Consider the opening of the second movement of Mozart's Piano Concerto in A Major, K. 488 (shown in Example 1.2).

One might begin a discussion of the piece with the sentence:

Slow pieces in minor keys always make me feel sad.

But this alerts the reader to two unfortunate things:

- The author is more interested in his or her own opinions and feelings than in the work itself.
- An entire discussion is about to be based on a bland, naive, and highly personal statement.

Our author has thus broken one of the most basic rules of writing: *never* make the reader doubt your ability. A related situation occurs when a live performer inadvertently plants doubts in the mind of the audience, through inappropriate concert behavior, apparent nervousness, technical inaccuracies, or memory lapses; since no one wants to feel insecure on another's behalf, the instinct is to exit the performance out of embarrassment for the performer. The reader's mode of exit is to turn the page or put down the work altogether.

Yet the fact that the concerto movement is slow and in a minor key *is* relevant to the mood Mozart is trying to project, and our fictitious author's response may be close to that which Mozart intended. How, then, might we rewrite the sentence to use the obviously good instincts shown in the disastrous first version in a more effective and promising way? Perhaps:

> The second movement's slow tempo and minor key seem sad and poignant, particularly after the sweetness and brilliance of the first movement.

This version makes a similar point, but it offers musical evidence (that is, the comparison to what was heard immediately before) and it is put in a far less personal way. It speaks about the same melancholy musical effect, places it in the context of the previous movement, and uses as evidence what previously had been mere stimuli for authorial musings. Put this way, it makes a persuasive argument: almost any listener to Western concert and popular music knows, instinctively or from study, that—particularly in the eighteenth century—minor keys and slow tempi frequently have associations of sadness or drama.

A more detailed treatment of the opening might address the choice of F-sharp minor specifically, the harmonic language, the melodic intervals, the traditional associations of the underlying dance type (Siciliano), and any number of other aspects, in order to strengthen the same point. But in most cases additional details would be unnecessary; two aspects of the music, clear and easy to hear, can be used to explain the listener's response. The fact that this response is not prefaced with "I feel that" and supported by "I just *hear* it that way," and that it is based on characteristics inherent in the music, makes it no less an opinion, and no more a "fact." Opinion is present, but the reader knows that there is more support than authorial whim.

Because music is a nonverbal, largely nonrepresentative art, there sometimes seems to be little of a concrete nature about it, and it can prove to be a maddeningly elusive subject for an author. But we have seen that there are many ways to write about music, so there is no single right answer waiting to be discovered. What remains is to begin, and to begin without fear.

You are reading this book because of a commitment to music. This book will offer guidance, but you need to be reading indefatigably about music elsewhere and learning to identify good, meaningful, economical writing—writing upon which you can begin to model your own efforts. The same passion and drive that motivate you to practice, perform, compose, and teach music, or even just to listen to it and learn more about it, should also motivate you to improve your writing about it. Make it concise, make it elegant, make it compelling. Finally, be prepared to make mistakes. Mere avoidance of errors is no goal. Write freely but self-evaluate brutally, and strive not to repeat your mistakes. The result will be writing that is gratifying both to read and to digest.

2

WRITING ABOUT MUSIC BY, AND FOR, THOSE WHO CANNOT (NECESSARILY) READ IT

Most rock musicians lack formal musical training, and so do almost all rock commentators. They lack the vocabulary and techniques of musical analysis, and even the descriptive words that critics and fans do use—harmony, melody, riff, beat—are only loosely understood and applied. I share this ignorance . . . [1]

—SIMON FRITH

For most kinds of musical writing, it is highly desirable and always advantageous to be not just an experienced listener but musically literate.[2] Whether one is writing reviews, publicity, or opinion, the technical knowledge of written musical language is irreplaceable; the musically literate author can elucidate or respond to musical works and performances with collegial empathy in a way unavailable to one who simply listens "from the outside." (Ideally, some performance experience—that is, rendering written musical

---

[1]Simon Frith, *Sound Effects: Youth, Leisure, and the Politics of Rock 'N' Roll* (New York: Pantheon Books, 1982), 13.
[2]The ability to read music is an absolute requirement for the analysis and detailed discussion of musical content. This task will be addressed in Chapter 3.

symbols into living, breathing musical experiences—is highly desirable also.) The more experience a writer has with a subject, after all, the better informed the writing! Individuals with an ongoing commitment to effective writing about music must therefore seek musical instruction and experience, if they do not yet have it, so as to be fully prepared for the task.

Unarmed but overly ambitious authors require only a few words to embarrass themselves: "The album has a floating feeling. There is a high, motionless motion, and John shows his ability to play romance . . . "[3] Does the album *have* a floating feeling (do albums have feelings?) or is this how this one listener felt upon hearing it? What *is* "motionless motion," anyway? Note also a tendency to be overly familiar, common in jazz and popular music criticism, by referring to artists by their first names. In sum, the risk of writing something as windily meaningless as this description of jazz giant John Coltrane is simply too great to allow the wise writer to enter the ring unprepared.

That said, there are kinds of writing for which musical literacy is not a prerequisite. One kind of response to music's ability to excite the imagination consists of writing that utilizes elements of the fantastic. Consider the following passage from E. M. Forster's *Howards End*, in which the reader hears the close of Beethoven's Fifth Symphony through the ears of a highly intelligent and passionate young girl:

> . . . as if things were going too far, Beethoven took hold of the goblins and made them do what he wanted. He appeared in person. He gave them a little push, and they began to walk in major key instead of in a minor, and then—he blew with his mouth, and they were scattered! Gusts of splendor, gods and demi-gods contending with vast swords, color and fragrance broadcast on the field of battle, magnificent victory, magnificent death! . . . Any fate was titanic; any contest desirable; conqueror and conquered would alike be applauded by the angels of the utmost stars. . . .
>
> Beethoven chose to make all right in the end. He blew with his mouth for the second time, and again the goblins were scattered. He brought back the gusts of splendor, the heroism, the youth, the magnificence of life and of death, and, amid vast roarings of a superhuman joy, he led his Fifth Symphony to its conclusion. But the goblins were there.

[3]Cuthbert O. Simpkins, quoted in V. J. Panetta's review of Eric Nisenson's *Ascension: John Coltrane and His Quest, Notes* 52/1 (September 1995), 118.

They could return. He had said so bravely, and that is why one can trust Beethoven when he says other things.[4]

Writing such as this is best reserved for literature, not analysis or review. Nonetheless it illustrates how evocative nontechnical writing can be, and how subjective, untrained, and frankly emotional responses can suggest a musical mood or experience in a way that no amount of terminological precision can. (Note the way a deft reference to the archaic English of the King James Bible—"he blew with his mouth"—lends a sense of epic timelessness to the girl's fantasy.) As music itself is not usually composed with specialists in mind, such naive but impassioned reactions as that of Forster's character may well suggest successful, direct emotional communication of the kind many composers want to have with their listeners.

The use of imagery may also effectively set the stage for a more in-depth discussion. The following passage introduces a detailed treatment of a popular and accessible work by Johann Strauss. The encapsulation of its opening mood through a few everyday images is highly effective as an introduction to the detail of the later discussion of structure, musical materials, and compositional procedure.

> The first sounds we hear in Johann Strauss's *Emperor Waltz* are surely those of marching, rather than dancing, feet. The steady alternation—one, two, one, two—of soft string chords leads to a modest tune, its lightly military rhythm underlined by the rustle of the snare drum. Four bars in the woodwinds are answered by a pendant in the violins, then repeated in a slightly fuller setting (with the merest *soupçon* of a martial gesture from the trumpet), answered by a different pendant. Indubitably a march, but on a very special scale: perhaps a bird's-eye view of the parade ground, or toy soldiers at drill—the specific metaphor doesn't really matter, rather the sense of distance and of proportion that it conveys.[5]

No technical jargon (other than counting beats: one-two, one-two) is used here, but the musical character is clear. This is not an independent passage, though; it prepares the reader for the analysis that follows. While it ably illustrates a nontechnical approach, we need to ask what *self-standing* kinds of writing may successfully be done by those with no academic knowledge of music. For these authors, the potential vulnerabilities require a careful choice of tasks and circumstances.

[4]Edward Morgan Forster, *Howards End* [1910] (New York, Alfred A. Knopf, 1951), 40–41. British spellings have been Americanized.
[5]David Hamilton, "The Secret Life of a Waltz," *High Fidelity* (October 1975), 36.

WHAT YOU CAN AND CANNOT DO

The primary responsibility of any writer is to know what he or she is talking about. We tend to assume that the authors we read have sufficient background, and we are disappointed when, for example, musical terminology is misused. Words such as *form, harmony,* and *counterpoint* have explicit musical meanings that are not identical to their general meanings in nonmusical contexts (a point made by Simon Frith in the quotation that heads this chapter). It is fair to say that if an author has no clear, specific understanding of how music works, then all analysis and use of musical terminology is off limits. That author simply does not have the tools to complete the job, and will end up making a mess of it with pretentious and ignorant writing. Here is an example from a New York newspaper:

> Interwoven throughout Falla's music were the Phoenician modal effects of flamenco's 12-count *bulerias* on the symphonic line. Flamenco's *cante jondo* lived in [the singer's] voice as she transformed *El amor brujo* into an Andalusian creole. With [the dancer] embodying Falla's score, both women performed the intertext of Spanish and gypsy, paying homage to women performers in modernist style.[6]

This passage is prodigiously silly. After loosing a salvo of random musical terms, the author suddenly switches to a tone of specialized (but barely understood) academic criticism: *cante jondo* (deep song—a flamenco style) "living in" the singer's voice, the dancer's "embodying" Falla's score, "performing the intertext," and so on. Not only do the three clauses of the final sentence seem unrelated to one another, but "gypsy" remains uncapitalized—an ethnic insult in an effusive discussion of a style of music and dance in which Kalo Gypsies played a formative role. ("Roma" is preferable to "Gypsies," but that would require further discussion.) Most outrageously, the author pretends to understand enough of the music of the ancient Phoenicians (the ancestors of the modern-day Lebanese, whose music does not survive in any traceable form) to identify the presence of its modes in a flamenco work.

It is thus apparent that musical detail, even in a nonanalytical context, is no area for novices. Because most people love music, writers tend to assume they can write about it on a technical level for which they are in fact manifestly unequipped. The author with only general knowledge

[6]Ninotchka Bennahum, "Musical Modernismo," *The Village Voice,* 1 April 1997, 83.

will not succeed when writing requires specificity of description and comprehension. In sum: if you do not thoroughly understand it, do not attempt to write about it.

What does this leave? Actually, a good deal.

THE CONCERT REVIEW

Every musician dreads a review by the musically inexperienced writer, but musical experience need not involve music literacy. One can maintain a lifetime's interest in music, with a long history of concert attendance and a large collection of recordings, perhaps even singing in a church or community choir and playing in folk- or popular-music groups, and still not have acquired musical literacy. The fundamental issues in review writing involve the reviewer's audience, goals, intent, and morality. The best preparation for reviewing, especially the reviewing of classical concerts, is a knowledge of and experience with the repertoire being performed. Mere musical literacy is no guarantee of this, and indeed it can often mislead a reviewer into thinking he or she knows more than may be the case. What, before we go further, is the purpose of a concert review? It is multifaceted, and its focus depends on the publication in which it appears (or the nature of the assignment) and its audience.

Reporting on a News Event

Musicians almost universally regard concert reviews with suspicion and hostility, often on the basis of bad personal experience. But in most situations, a primary function of the review is reportage, informing the readership of a newspaper or magazine about an arts event that took place in the community. Relatively few communities have an individual with advanced musical expertise who is willing or able to write *what* the newspaper editor wants, *when* he or she wants it (usually late the same evening that the concert took place), for the available amount of money (usually negligible). Accordingly, many concert reviews are written by people whose chief qualification is a general interest in the arts. Such reviews may consist of discussion of the works performed, some evaluation of the performers, and description of the general effect upon audience and reviewer. Given the nature of both writer and audience, the question of tone is all-important.

In most places, concert music and the other arts are supported by a small minority. Accordingly, a spirit of appreciation, with the idea of inspiring broader interest in music in general, is an appropriate starting point for the reviewer. It is an unhappy fact that certain reviewers, taking advantage of the fact that their words will be read in the following day's newspaper, relish sitting in merciless judgment on the musicians they review. No example of this destructive and entirely inappropriate writing is needed here; its character is unmistakable.

This is not to say that performers never deserve censure. Even under the most stressful and irregular performing circumstances, the audience must be respected, regardless of excessive coughing or other misbehavior. (The matter of applauding between movements is more problematic; considered ignorant and gauche today, it was historically not only appropriate but common courtesy.) When issues of competence or professionalism are raised—say, if the technical flaws in a performance multiply to the point of eclipsing all other aspects, or if a performer shows disdain for the audience or other performers—then it is the responsibility of the reviewer to address them directly, since they lie at the heart of artistic communication. Initial goodwill in the reviewer need not, in this unfortunate circumstance, become a governing principle or requirement. The performer has earned, by charging admission for a musical performance but not executing professional responsibilities, whatever rebuke the reviewer has to offer. Fortunately, such cases are rare.

The best mindset for reviewers is a positive and appreciative one that brings a benignly neutral attitude to each performance.

Artistic Evaluation

Going beyond simple reportage, why would one evaluate a musical performance? For precisely the same reasons one would review a movie or play: so that those not present may have some idea of what was missed, and so that they may consider attending performances by the same performers (or of the same works, or of works by the same composers). Artistic evaluation examines the components of the performance, which include technical mastery, interpretive concept, style awareness, and the ability to communicate and move the audience. Each of these is, to some extent, subjective: technical mastery is obvious on a basic level, but beyond that level, criteria can be highly individual. An interpretive concept may be obvious to one listener and mystifying to another (and it can be a matter of taste). Style awareness is a matter of informed debate, and the ability to communicate with a listener is ultimately a personal judgment. A reviewer cannot pretend to speak for others' perceptions, regardless of how representative of the readership he or she feels, but still should not write from a position too distant from that of most of the readership. Matters of precise musical detail are best left for scholarly articles and conversation among musicians. Treating such specifics in a review is impractical and therefore inadvisable.

A good writer is nonetheless able to convey a great deal of information about a performer's artistry using nontechnical language, and in doing so communicate to readers on a variety of levels. Take, for example, this excerpt from Virgil Thomson's review of the cellist Pierre Fournier's American debut in New York (the review appeared in the *New York Herald* on November 14, 1948):

> Excellence in the technical handling of the cello is always primarily a matter of avoiding pitfalls. Mr. Fournier does not let his instrument groan or scratch or squeak or buzz, and yesterday he did not miss exact pitch on more than just a very few notes. Neither did he at any time force his tone beyond the volume of optimum sonority. His sound, in consequence, was always pleasant and, thanks to Mr. Fournier's fine musical sensitivity, extremely varied.
>
> That sensitivity was present in positive form, moreover, as liveness of rhythm and in the wonderful shaping and shading of each line and phrase. Many cellists can play with dignity and style, as Mr. Fournier did, an unaccompanied Bach suite; but few can play a Brahms sonata, as he did yesterday the F major, with such buoyancy and spontaneity, such grace of feeling and no heaviness at all. I know of none who can match him in the Debussy Sonata.
>
> This work is rather a rhapsody than a sonata in the classical sense, and yet it needs in execution a sonata's continuous flow and long-line planning. It needs also the utmost of delicacy and of variety in coloration and a feeling of freedom in its rhythmic progress. Its performance yesterday by Mr. Fournier and his accompanist, George Reeves, was a high point in a season already notable for good ensemble work . . . [7]

There is not one sentence in this excerpt, from those addressing technical mastery, the shaping and shading of phrases, or interpretive

---

[7]Virgil Thomson, from "Virtuoso Makes Music," which originally appeared on November 14, 1948. It is reprinted in Thomson, *Music Right and Left* (New York: Henry Holt and Company, 1951), 43.

flow and long-line planning, that would not be comprehensible to any music lover, whether musically literate or not. Of course, Virgil Thomson, an important twentieth-century American composer and music critic, was musically literate. But in the reviewing process, one is rarely called upon to display one's learning, and Thomson does not. He looks for the best, in this review, and is not disappointed. Moreover, he honors the collaborating artist by acknowledging him by name (which is *always* the right thing to do) rather than equating him with the stage crew by leaving him nameless.

Here is another example, from a review by Dawn Kummer, an undergraduate violinist at the time it was written, of a faculty composition concert. She focuses not on the performance but on the work, which she has never heard before, and uses little or no technical terminology both to describe the interaction between musical and nonmusical media and to give a good sense of the work as a whole.

This program had two highlights. The first was *Images From the Edge of Time* by John McLaird, a piece inspired by pictures sent back to Earth by the Hubble space telescope. McLaird compiled these images into three short segments of film, then wrote the music to accompany them. Although the music could stand on its own, I greatly enjoyed the visual as well as the aural experience. The first segment was titled "Galaxies and Stars." The music was busy sounding, with many rapidly-moving passages. It perfectly matched images bursting with light and color. The second was "Novae and Nebulae: The Birth and Death of Stars." The music here was slower and more solemn, befitting the wonder and gravity of the subject. The final segment, "Images From the Edge of Time: Pictures of Different Objects," was more contrapuntal. This piece was written for full orchestra, although its performance here was entirely synthesized. Except for the extremes of range (especially in the last movement), the difference was barely noticeable.

Ms. Kummer's description touches on a variety of aspects of the piece, including the inspiration for its composition, the multimedia approach taken by the composer, the musical contrasts between the three movements, and the performing forces, both as conceived and as realized in this particular performance. The only specifically musical concepts here are range and contrapuntal texture, which would be familiar to any music appreciation student. The result is that her writing would make sense to virtually any reader.

To sum up: although music literacy is desirable in writing concert reviews, without it a great deal may still be communicated, because there is no literacy requirement for *readers* of reviews. Far more important for the reviewing process are perceptive listening, an understanding of one's audience, and a good sense for the kind of information they will be prepared to understand.

Promoting Community Interest in Music

To promote a community's interest in music is an important goal of many concert reviews, particularly those written in places that are not urban musical centers, and it would be disingenuous to act as if only higher artistic considerations were relevant. Of this promotional aspect, little need be said other than to reassure reviewers that they need not sacrifice authorial integrity. Putting live musical activity in a favorable light (or in as favorable a light as possible) will in most cases serve the greater good: more community awareness of, and interest in, live music. Enumerating a performer's technical flaws, questionable interpretive decisions, or relative lack of experience will not advance this goal, and in general it is the positive aspects of a performance that should receive the most attention anyway. This is not to say that the review should be mere publicity fluff; it is simply wise to remember that a positive outlook will be far preferable, for a local audience, to bitter criticism of local artists or anecdotes of higher standards in urban centers. Again: always remember for whom you write, and why.

POPULAR AND WORLD MUSICS

Whether music literacy, or indeed musical training of any other kind, is needed to write about popular and world musics is an open question. ("World music" is itself becoming a contested term, and has come to denote traditional—that is, folk—musics of the world, "classical" or art musics of cultures outside the West, popular or entertainment musics from anywhere, and especially free blends of all these musics and Western art or popular music elements.) Popular and world musics are in some ways similar, as for example in the way that both repertories are part of the everyday experiences of millions, probably billions, of musically nonliterate people. Often the performers themselves can neither read nor write music, so it would seem odd to require musical literacy and academic training of those writing about such music. Some people find, however, a degree of ethnocentricity in the position that Western classical music somehow requires potential authors to have a kind of background that popular and world musics do not. Although Western musical literacy is relevant especially for Western classical music, many believe that thorough academic training is necessary to write responsibly about *any* music, that there is neither inherent irony nor contradiction in enjoying far more training than your musical subject, since your jobs are different. Ultimately, it depends on the individual case: the amount of training the author needs will depend on what specifically about the music is to be discussed. Much writing about popular and world musics does not require musical literacy. An example of the kind that does will be found in Chapter 3.

The quotation from Simon Frith that heads this chapter makes an important point. Frith is one of England's most prominent rock writers, and his statement about many rock musicians' lack of technical vocabulary is certainly true. (A case in point is ex-Beatle Paul McCartney, a fine electric bassist, one of the most famous songwriters in history, and composer of at least two works of art music, *Liverpool Oratorio* and *Standing Stones*. Until at least the early 1990s he was, by his own very public admission, musically illiterate.) Frith, a sociologist, tends to address rock music's place in society, the elements of listeners' culture and collective psyche it touches, and the commercial aspects of the rock market. For these subjects, musical literacy is unnecessary, as it would probably be in similar discussions relating to classical music. To expect more of authors and readers than of the musicians themselves, in such cases as these, seems pointlessly elitist—a latter-day echo of the Roman author Boethius, who felt that the only true musicians were judges and critics, whereas the performers and composers who made the music were little more than slaves and artisans.

A passage from Edward Macan's discussion of the album *Tarkus*, by the 1970s progressive-rock band Emerson, Lake and Palmer, illustrates how much can be communicated without the use of academic terminology.

> The most impressive musical achievement of *Tarkus* is the effective tension maintained between impetuous, improvisatory sections and coherent long-range planning. Besides effectively juxtaposing different

approaches to tempo, instrumentation, and harmony, *Tarkus* also makes effective use of contrasts in melodic character; the rhythmically smooth, stepwise vocal lines of the second and sixth movements can be contrasted with the jagged, rhythmically irregular motives of movements one, three, and five or the short, incantatory themes of the movements four and seven. Contrasts in meter play a role as well, since the instrumental movements tend toward unusual meters (the first and third movements are in five), while the "song" movements are all in common time (i.e., four).[8]

Macan, writing a book for a nonspecialist audience, here provides an overview of the pacing of the album as a whole. He compares the various movements with regard to melodic language (conjunct or "stepwise" melody being a basic concept), rhythmic character, and meter (for which the only technical knowledge required is the ability to count beats and sense accents). Macan, a trained musicologist, is of course literate, but music literacy is unnecessary for the audience he seeks to reach.

That said, it is also undeniable that the discussion of rock songs (like other artworks, popular and otherwise) often requires specialized terminology, and whether or not the artist would understand that terminology is irrelevant. An example of this is the excerpt from Matthew Brown's analysis of Jimi Hendrix's song "Little Wing," which appears in Chapter 3; precise knowledge of musical terminology and the ability to mentally "hear" chord progressions are prerequisites for understanding the writing. Although the music is fairly nontraditional (academically speaking, at least), the discussion is squarely within standard analytical boundaries, and comprehension of it is virtually impossible without full music literacy.

Depending on the author's point, the reader's need for academic background can go beyond basic musical training. Consider Robert Walser's critical commentary on the song "Heaven Sent," by the heavy metal band Dokken:

> The guitar solo, often the site of virtuosic transcendence of a metal song's constructions of power and control, is, in "Heaven Sent," a veritable catalog of the musical semiotics of doom. As with "ground bass" patterns in seventeenth-century opera, the harmonic pattern uses cyclicism to suggest fatefulness; as in certain of Bach's keyboard pieces, the

[8]Edward Macan, *Rocking the Classics* (New York and Oxford: Oxford University Press, 1997), 94.

virtuoso responds to the threat of breakdown with irrational, frenzied chromatic patterns. The guitar solo is an articulation of frantic terror, made all the more effective by its technical impressiveness and its imitations of vocal sounds such as screams and moans. After the solo, the song's chorus intensifies these images through ellision [sic]: seven measures long instead of the normal, balanced eight, the pattern cycles fatalistically, without rest or resolution.[9]

Such concepts as elided seven-bar phrases, chromaticism, and ground basses are probably foreign to readers who have not had systematic music study, and the comparisons with seventeenth-century opera and Bach's keyboard works would elude many who have not studied the history of Western art music. Beyond that, Walser draws heavily on another specialized academic vocabulary: such ideas as "the constructions of power and control" and "the semiotics of doom" are likely to puzzle readers unfamiliar with the rhetoric of the critical disciplines. Clearly, this kind of writing is targeted at a specific, relatively narrow audience (that is, academics with an interest in music); those without musical training and a good deal of experience with academic discourse are simply not equipped to understand this kind of cross-disciplinary approach.

The world of rock and pop journalism presents a different set of circumstances. A rather large percentage of rock journalism does not seek to discuss the music, but rather the performative aspects, the reactions of writer and/or crowd, and the lifestyle associated with the music—often dwelling on the backstage, touring, and business scenes. More to our purposes, when the actual music is discussed, the Dionysian and celebrative aspects of the music can be (though are not always) reflected in the writing. Critic Lester Bangs here offers this credo:

Rock and roll is an attitude, and if you've got the attitude you can do it, no matter what anybody says. . . . Rock is for everybody[;] it should be so implicitly anti-élitist that the question of whether somebody's qualified to perform it should never arise.

But it did. In the sixties, of course . . . in the sixties rock and roll began to think of itself as an "art-form." Rock & roll is not an "art-form;" rock and roll is a raw wail from the bottom of the guts.[10]

[9]Robert Walser, *Running with the Devil: Power, Gender, and Madness in Heavy Metal Music* (Hanover, NH and London: Wesleyan University Press, 1993), 119.
[10]"In Which Another Pompous Blowhard Purports to Possess the True Meaning of Punk Rock," copyright Lester Bangs, 1980. Used by permission of Raines and Raines for the Lester Bangs Estate.

Whether or not one is in real sympathy with him, it is hard *not* to know what he means. In rock writing, more literary excesses are and have always been tolerated. Nonetheless, the author's personal touch can still be excessive. Here, Nick Kent deals directly with the song "Marquee Moon" by the band by Television (written by singer Tom Verlaine). The results are chaotic at best, as Kent slips helplessly from a description of the lyrical imagery to his own free association to a wan stab at the song's structure and musical language.

> Slowly a story unfurls—a typically surreal Verlaine ghost story involving Cadillacs pulling up in graveyards and disembodied arms beckoning the singer to get in while "lightning struck itself," and various twilight rejects from *King Lear* (that last bit's my own flight of fancy, by the way), babbling crazy retorts to equally crazy questions. The lyrics as a scenario for the music are utterly compelling. The song's structure is unlike anything I've ever heard before. It transforms from a strident two-chord construction, to a breath-takingly beautiful chord progression, which acts as a motif/climax for the narrative, as the song ends with a majestic chord pattern.[11]

Points granted for passion, but the only actual content is the vague discussion of the lyrics; the rest is largely Kent's self-indulgence— "majestic chord pattern," after all, does not tell us very much. But in writing as in all other human endeavor, risks sometimes pay off, and the stylistic excesses in rock journalism can result in compelling and vivid prose. Here is an excerpt from "A Posthumous Interview," in which Lester Bangs makes as if to interview Jimi Hendrix after the latter's gruesome death following a drug overdose. In one of the most restrained passages in the "interview" (really!), he has Hendrix hold forth on the quality of his own music. Note: virtually no technical knowledge of music would be necessary to read or understand this, but it could not have been written without Bangs's intimate knowledge of Hendrix's work, blues per se, other blues players, and other popular musics of the time. Music literacy is not required for this kind of writing, in other words, but command of the subject—real expertise—is; this is not the writing of a novice or dilettante. In this passage, Bangs-as-"interviewer" has just asked

---

[11]Nick Kent, review of "Marquee Moon" by the band Television, *New Musical Express* 5, February 1977. Permission for use kindly granted by NME.

Hendrix's spirit about such songs as "Red House" and "Voodoo Chile"—"They were incredible songs, fantastically played!" "Hendrix" responds:

> They weren't exactly what you would call original compositions. They were good takes, especially the second "Voodoo Chile." The long version had a nice feel, but it was there to fill out a double album, and Winwood played the same damn solo he played on "Pearly Queen" and every other damn session he did for about three years. I played good blues on "Red House," but it got way more attention than it deserved, probably because it was so hard to get in America for a long time. I mean, "I Don't Live Today" is real blues, modern blues—it's what happens when you drop a hydrogen bomb on the blues, which is what it deserves.
>
> Listen. The blues is white music, and so was most "free jazz." All the musicians know it, everybody in the ghetto knows it because they'd be boppin' to James Brown and Stanley Turrentine, don't own Muddy Waters albums much less Robert Johnson, and 98 per cent of 'em never heard of Albert Ayler. My music was at least 70 per cent white. If I'd played what black people wanted to hear at that time I'da been spectacularly unsuccessful in the hip rock superstar world, and if I'd gone down to the Apollo Theater and played what I played at the Fillmore I probably woulda been laughed off the stage. And knowing that has dogged my ass all the way to this moment.[12]

Even the few examples of popular-music writing given here illustrate the central point: the authorial decisions necessary for writing about music are even more critical when writing about rock and pop. At the very earliest stages, the author must consider who the audience is, what kinds of musical background they have already, what points must be made, and what stylistic approach would best serve. Writing about popular music can range from the most specialized academic prose to measured explanation and analysis to Dionysian effusion and creative writing, and depending on the situation and readership all these styles can be completely appropriate. Remember the corollary, though: all can be completely *in*appropriate. *Caveat auctor.*

---

[12]"Jimi Hendrix: A Posthumous Interview with Lester Bangs" was originally published in *CREEM* Magazine, April 1976. Used with permission, CREEMMagazine.com.

Crossing the Cultural Divide

World musics—traditional and cultivated alike—pose problems similar to those of popular music. A typical assignment in world music courses, particularly introductory ones, is the basic exploratory paper, which might address the musical instruments and the musical language of another culture, and the uses and situation of music within that culture. For this (and depending on the depth of the inquiry), musical literacy may not be necessary; an author can provide an overview of a foreign music and its instruments without providing in-depth analysis and musical examples. Indeed, the ethnomusicologist Bruno Nettl observes:

> The world's tribal musical cultures . . . have less in the way of music theory and of professionalization of musicians, and they have no musical notation. Quantitatively, their musics are simpler than the art musics of the world.[13]

This observation (which Nettl follows with the counterexample of African rhythmic structures) will only go so far. It may briefly reassure an author with no musical literacy, but musical literacy itself (especially if "literacy" refers only to the standard Western notational system) may be largely irrelevant to the musical culture in question. All musicians acknowledge the gap between musical notation and the music *itself* that notation seeks to record, or that is realized from it; although this gap is perceived to be large in Western classical music, for most other musics it is far greater.

Our reliance on our inherited form of notation weights our understanding of music in favor of those aspects that are readily notatable, and it places those that are less so at a substantial disadvantage. Richard Middleton illustrates this shaping of our musical thought and perception in his identification of the difficulties in applying standard musical vocabulary to popular music—and it is even truer for world musics. Since Western art music is notation-based, our terminology enables us to talk best about such aspects of music as pitch, harmony, and meter, but it puts us at a disadvantage when we discuss

> . . . non-standard pitch and non-discrete pitch movement (slides, slurs, blue notes, microtones, and so on); irregular, irrational rhythms,

---

[13]Bruno Nettl, *Folk and Traditional Music of the Western Continents* [1965] (Englewood Cliffs, NJ: Prentice-Hall, 1990), 1–2.

polyrhythms, and rhythmic nuance (off-beat phrasing, slight delays, anticipations and speed-ups, and the complex durational relationships often involved in heterophonic and "loose" part-playing, and overlapping antiphonal phrases); nuances of ornamentation, accent, articulation (attack, sustain, decay: what electronic musicians and sound engineers call the "envelope") and performer idiolect; specificities (as opposed to abstractions) of timbre . . . [14]

So, even full Western musical literacy does not necessarily equip an author to write easily about many aspects of popular music, and with world musics the picture is complicated by completely different theoretical (codified or not), practical, pedagogical, and aesthetic principles. Does a responsible author attempt to write about Indian classical music without a solid knowledge of what a *raga* is, or Arabic music without a knowledge of the *maqam*? Does a knowledge of Western musical theory allow us to discuss the many subtle ways in which music, in many cultures, is understood to connect this world with the spirit realm? How can we engage in a comprehensible discussion of the specifics of a music that cannot practically be adapted to our notational system? Especially for non-Western musics, moreover, isn't *cultural* literacy a more crucial prerequisite for enabling an author to write about an unfamiliar music for a Western readership?

For these musics, authors need training of a different kind, perhaps (or perhaps not) involving musical notation—that of Western music or any other kind. What will also be necessary is some understanding of anthropology, and more specifically of the conceptual background and vocabulary of the relevant culture. Ethnomusicology, the discipline that studies traditional musics of other countries and cultures (and, more recently, vernacular traditions and music sociologies in various Western cultures, too), comprises a variety of disciplines, borrowing methodologies from anthropology, history, sociology, cultural studies—especially critical techniques for "reading" economic, marketing, and propaganda phenomena—and others. Anthropologist Christopher A. Waterman suggests that

adequate accounts of musical continuity and change must deal, to the extent that sources and scholarly competence allow, with relationships among patterns of musical sound and performance behavior, cultural

[14]Richard Middleton, *Studying Popular Music* (Philadelphia: Open University Press, 1990), 104–05.

symbolism and value, societal transaction and ideology, and the material forces that encourage or constrain particular forms of expression.[15]

More directly, Karin Barber, a scholar of West African Studies, says that "the arts cannot be 'read' without *both* comprehending their nature as aesthetic constructs with their own principles and conventions, *and* locating them in the specific societal universe which is the grounds of their existence."[16] Expertise beyond music is therefore clearly required.

An elegant example of the balancing act between musical description and cultural significance is found is the following discussion, by David Goldsworthy, of the role of the big gong in Javanese gamelan music:

> On the other hand, the gong represents and expresses the timeless, diffuse, undefined and ambiguous nature of the *gamelan* world. Several factors contribute to this. Firstly, the practice of momentarily suspending metronomic time—called *elastic* or *breath rhythm* by some scholars (for example, in relation to Japanese *gagaku* music[17])—is commonly employed in Java by slightly delaying the gong stroke at the end of each cycle. This momentary but perceptible retardation could be regarded as negating the gong's accepted role as a definitive time marker, and contributing to a sense of the illusion of "real" time. Timelessness is also a factor after the gong stroke, because a gong stroke is not in reality a single discrete event with a definite duration. It is not usually damped by the performer and so continues to vibrate for some time after it is struck—how long depends on the acoustic characteristics of the gong itself and how it is struck. Thus a gong stroke cannot be defined as a precise moment in time, but rather constitutes a period of time. Moreover, the continuing vibration of the gong after it is struck has a rhythm of its own which is not necessarily that of the other instruments; this contributes to temporal ambiguity and confirms the gong's dual function of indicating time and "timelessness."[18]

[15]Christopher A. Waterman, "*Jùjú* History: Toward a Theory of Sociomusical Practice," in *Ethnomusicology and Modern Music History*, ed. Stephen Blum, Philip V. Bohlman, and Daniel M. Neuman (Urbana and Chicago: University of Illinois Press, 1991), 50.

[16]Karin Barber, "Popular Arts in Africa," *African Studies Review* 30/3 (September 1987), 5.

[17]William P. Malm, *Music Cultures of the Pacific, the Near East, and Asia* (Upper Saddle River, NJ: Prentice Hall, 1967), 139.

[18]David Goldsworthy, "Cyclic Properties of Indonesian Music," *The Journal of Musicological Research* 24/3–4 (July–December 2005), 313–14.

Goldsworthy gives the reader a sense of not only the musical matter under discussion (the gong, how the gong is delayed, how it continues to vibrate), but also the way it is heard and what it means. Even so, given the use of specialized terms and the need for cultural context, probably less than half of this passage is actually *about the music*. Given the necessities of the subject at hand, it is probably unavoidable, but it does serve to raise the question of whether such writing is more about music or culture, and how far "writing about music" is the operative model for this kind of study.

More recently, ethnomusicological and ethnographic strategies are being used to look at *all* musics, not just traditional ones: popular, "world," and even cultivated art musics like Western classical music. As with traditional musics, the discussion changes dramatically when it is primarily peoples, cultures, and practices that are the focus of the discussion, as opposed to the music itself. It serves to illustrate that a more detailed treatment of persuasive writing about music that requires substantial polycultural literacies lies beyond the scope of this book.

This distinction between general, introductory writing and more detailed, informed writing is an important one. The former may be done without a substantial amount of prior training, but the latter requires it. The question of context mentioned at the beginning of this section thus remains: although it is wrong to imagine that someone without Western music literacy will be able to write anything of value about popular or world musics, it is also a mistake to think that these musics, because of (in some cases) their relative simplicity or (in others) their remoteness from Western conceptions, may safely be written about without sufficient preparation and experience.

To summarize this chapter, the kinds of writing that may successfully be done without the benefit of music literacy include:

- literary impressions
- reviews
- response papers
- certain kinds of writing about primarily oral traditions (rock, world musics, etc.) but with the greatest possible care

To this list may be added other kinds of writing addressed elsewhere in this book:

- publicity notices
- article summaries and abstracts, given sufficient comprehension

The primary requirements for writing about music are clear listening and thinking, knowledge of one's audience, and an awareness of one's own limitations. For those intending ongoing activity in Western music (beyond rock and pop), acquiring music literacy and systematic music training are necessary, while for those branching into non-Western and popular musics, the culture and type of music will define the academic preparation needed.

3

WRITING MUSIC ANALYSIS

In all compositions I endeavor to fathom the diverse impulses inspiring them and their inner life. Is not this much more interesting than the game of pulling them to pieces, like curious watches?[1]
—M. Croche the Dilettante Hater [Claude Debussy]

Don't quote 6/4 chords and so on in the text. I am the composer, and I don't understand.[2]

—César Cui

ANALYSIS AND ITS USES

I know of no more accurate or helpful definition of analysis than that of Ian Bent, from *The New Grove Dictionary of Music and Musicians:*

> The primary impulse of analysis is an empirical one: to get to grips with something on its own terms rather than in terms of other things. Its starting-point is a phenomenon itself rather than external factors (such as biographical facts, political events, social conditions, educational methods, and all the other factors that make up the environment of that phenomenon). . . .

[1]Claude Debussy, *Monsieur Croche the Dilettante Hater* [1905], in *Three Classics in the Aesthetic of Music* (New York: Dover, 1962), 5.
[2]César Cui, letter of 29 September 1893 to Semyon Kruglikov (translated by Lyle Neff). The Russian original may be found in *Izbrannye pis'ma,* ed. I. L. Gusin (Leningrad: State Music Publishers, 1955), 159.

Analysis is the means of answering directly the question "How does it work?"[3]

This is a traditionalist view. That is, many contemporary scholars would argue that the question "How does it work?" is incompletely answered when biographical facts, social conditions, and so on remain outside the discussion; they do, after all, have direct bearing on the way listeners hear and understand music, and therefore on how—and why—it works. But as Bent's definition stands, it addresses the workings of the piece itself, the way the musical materials are deployed and how they interrelate. This is precisely how analysis is usually understood.

Why analyze? Does this endeavor represent no more than disassembling musical works "like curious watches," as Debussy contemptuously suggested? Pulling music apart is a necessary part of analysis, but it is only the first step. The ability to think analytically about music is an absolute necessity for those who seek to understand, teach, interpret, and write about music, and—properly done—analysis has far more to do with "fathoming music's inner life" than it does with disassembly. Our primary concern is *writing* analysis; the acquisition of the necessary analytical vocabulary, background, and skills must take place in music theory and history courses.

Most analysis depends on printed score examples, as does the following discussion of the opening of the first movement of Mozart's Piano Concerto in A Major, K. 488 (shown in Example 3.1).

> The subtle poignancy of the G-natural in bar 1 is a master-stroke, as is the clash between G-sharp and A in the 4th beat of bar 2, and the less obvious dissonance between the chord of A major and the D in the bass in bar 4. It is these moments of harmonic tension that prevent the music from being merely bland; behind the sunny façade there are shadowy places.[4]

This excerpt from a longer analysis addresses how the passage "works" not by describing everything that happens, a good deal of which is obvious from the musical example, but rather by identifying those aspects that are noteworthy and therefore that contribute to a unique effect: the unexpected harmony (V^7/iv) caused by the G-natural, and the dissonances that follow in bars 2 and 4. The analyst expects the reader to

[3]Ian Bent, "Analysis," *The New Grove Dictionary of Music and Musicians,* 2nd ed., ed. Stanley Sadie (London: Macmillan, 2001), vol. 1, 527–28.
[4]Antony Hopkins, *Talking About Concertos* (London: Heinemann Educational Books, 1964), 25.

EX. 3.1
Mozart, Piano Concerto in A Major, K. 488, I, opening (piano reduction).

understand the eighteenth-century harmonic grammar in the musical example, but otherwise he offers no jargon or advanced analytical concepts. Some might find such figurative ideas as "poignancy," "sunny façade," and "shadowy places" to be outside the realm of pure analysis, but since they anchor Mozart's compositional choices to the way many hear and understand his music, their relevance to "how it works" is apparent. Analysis does not consist of simply listing characteristics or identifying particular gestures in a score example; it must show how these gestures relate to one another, how they work together to produce a composite effect and contribute to a coherent whole.

Analyses are often done in accordance with a specific system, such as traditional harmonic analysis, the linear analysis of Heinrich Schenker (illustrated by a characteristic kind of graphic representation[5]), or set

[5]Examples of Schenker's own analytical work may be found in Heinrich Schenker, *Five Graphic Musical Analyses* [1933], ed. Felix Salzer (New York: Dover, 1969). Example 3.4 also gives a Schenker graph.

theory. In each system, certain guidelines and analytical vocabulary are established at the outset, and the musical information is then interpreted within that context. Alternatively, analyses may be eclectic in approach, adhering to no particular model but rather seeking to clarify by whatever means seem appropriate. A certain amount of terminology is common to virtually all analytical approaches, so a solid background in music theory, in addition to complete musical literacy, is a prerequisite for both understanding and writing musical analyses.

ANALYTICAL CONTENT VS. PLAY-BY-PLAY

Example 3.2 gives the opening of the vocal part of Franz Schubert's *Der Hirt auf dem Felsen* (The Shepherd on the Rock) for voice, piano, and obbligato clarinet, op. 129 (D. 965).

As was the case with the Mozart analysis excerpted above, the presence of the musical example obviates the need for lengthy description, and the explanation of "how it works" can be focused on those aspects that are interesting or atypical. More obvious features may be pointed out when there is reason to do so, but they need not be described or explained. A treatment of this short passage might run this way:

> Noteworthy, here, is Schubert's treatment of the text. The opening line
> of the poem, "Wenn auf dem höchsten Fels ich steh" (When I stand on
> the highest cliff), is set to a stable piano accompaniment with unchang-
> ing texture and tonic-dominant harmonies. The melody makes use of
> word-painting: the "highest cliff" is suggested not only by the two iso-
> lated high F pitches but also by the disjunct "climbing" figures that lead

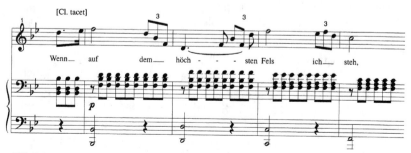

EX. 3.2
Schubert, *Der Hirt auf dem Felsen*, mm. 38–42.

up to them, thus showing how intimately a masterful vocal melody is bound up with the words it seeks to express.

The analyst has chosen to address the text-music relationship, which is central to any understanding of vocal music and in this case is particularly instructive. Other approaches might begin by commenting on the almost exclusive use of chord tones in the melody, or on its wide range, or on aspects of the rhythm and harmony. But the inclusion of a musical example enables the author to keep description to a minimum and to proceed to identifying important points. The cumulative effect is one of persuasion; the writer explains how the passage works using analytical arguments supported by reference to the score.

What will not pass for analysis is what I call play-by-play. Play-by-play, more a sign of inexperience than anything else, consists of detailed, literal narrative of what the notes are doing in a particular passage. A play-by-play treatment of the Schubert excerpt seen above in Example 3.2 might read this way:

> The melody, in $\frac{3}{4}$ time, begins on the upbeat with a dotted-eighth-note D and sixteenth-note E♭, a figure which leads up to a half-note F on the downbeat of the following bar. A descending triplet B♭ arpeggio on the third beat (D–B♭–F) leads down to a dotted-quarter-note D downbeat on the bar after, which—following an eighth-note F above it—ascends back up to the same high F through another arpeggiating triplet (this time, B♭–F–D). The phrase ends with an ornamental triplet on the third beat (E♭–F–D) that comes to rest on a C half-note below, on the following downbeat. The piano accompaniment is static—downbeat left-hand octaves followed by triplet chords in the right hand—and the harmony is equally unremarkable: two bars of the tonic followed by two of the dominant.

This passage is longer than the previous passage, says far less, and consists entirely of a recitation of musical events. Such a description is not necessarily an evil, but it needs to lead somewhere, which this example does not—it only duplicates the information found in the musical example. In the absence of a musical example, this kind of writing is tedious and thankless: few readers will have the patience or the ability to visualize or hum the line in their heads while they are reading. Occasionally a detailed play-by-play treatment of a particular passage may be necessary to establish, for purposes of the ensuing explanation, the precise nature of the musical elements or compositional choices; this is a common feature in major analyses, where an initial musical description will provide the fuel for pages of discussion. But for most student analyses, valuable space should not be devoted to material easily gleaned from a musical example. Following an analysis is never an effortless task, and so the author must write concisely, clearly, and meaningfully, doing everything possible to facilitate understanding.

Finally, valuable as musical examples are, they should be used judiciously; pages of score excerpts should not be allowed to swamp the explanation. Too many examples can produce an effect analogous to too many charts or graphs: the reader becomes impatient with having to jump repeatedly between the text and the accompanying music, and the thread of the argument becomes increasingly difficult to follow. A balance between explanatory words and illustrative musical examples, with a cold eye to the economical use of both, will point the way to effective analytical writing. (For information on how to incorporate musical examples in a manuscript, see Chapter 8.)

Analysis Without Musical Examples

Certain kinds of analysis do not require musical examples. Rock and many world musics are not notation-based (though they can certainly be notated), and it is not always helpful to render into notation, for purposes of analysis, what was not notated in any precise way in the first place. This passage from Matthew Brown's discussion of Jimi Hendrix's song "Little Wing" does not require an example:

> Most significantly, Hendrix's melodic and harmonic idiom also shows strong psychedelic influences. Whereas bars 1–4 are built from the familiar blues progression I–III–IV–I, bars 5–10 have quite different origins. For one thing, the overall motion from a B-minor chord (m. 5) through a C-major sonority (m. 8) to a D-major chord (mm. 9–10) is not typical of a blues in E; progressions of this type, with their weak tonal functions, are far more common in rock.[6] For another, the chromatic chords on B-flat and F in measures 5 and 7 are idiomatic of psychedelic music; both chords lie outside the prevailing pentatonic collection. Lastly, many of Hendrix's voicings are decidedly unbluesy. Most striking

---

[6][Author's footnote] Richard Bobbitt, *Harmonic Technique in the Rock Idiom* (Belmont, CA: Wadsworth, 1976), 92–110.

in this regard are the ubiquitous 4-3 and 9-8 suspensions and stacked fifths.[7]

Without relying on a musical example, Brown produces a clear, coherent analytical passage targeted at a musically trained readership. He uses standard musical terminology to discuss Hendrix's harmonic language, and although the reader may understand the differences between blues, rock, and psychedelic music (that last given only a vague treatment, unfortunately), Brown explains his observations anyway. To understand this passage, the reader must be able to "hear" a I-III-IV-I harmonic progression, and one from B minor to C to D; to understand how 4-3 and 9-8 suspensions work; and to know what stacked fifths and a pentatonic collection are. Musically trained readers who have some experience with rock music will be capable of "hearing" the harmony and understanding the discussion, but it is still true (and somewhat paradoxical) that musical analyses such as this, which do not use examples, require more of the reader, in certain ways, than those that do.

TECHNICAL TERMINOLOGY

The Hendrix analysis above illustrates that, whether a musical example is provided or not, you will need to use a certain amount of specific, technical vocabulary. Do not revel unnecessarily in technical language, but do not take heroic measures to avoid it; readers of musical analyses should be expected to understand it. For many general readers, concepts from undergraduate-level harmony class, such as Phrygian cadences and parallel fifths (or even dominant chords and dotted rhythms), will be incomprehensible. The same goes, only more so, for terms such as background, middleground, and foreground (in their music-specific senses), and for references to numbered pitch collections such as 014 trichords. Yet Schenker-based analysis is pointless without the former, and set theory depends on the latter. One of the main goals of classroom analysis is to demonstrate mastery of new concepts and vocabulary. Soft-pedaling such vocabulary and taking time and space for definitions are often counterproductive.

---

[7]Matthew Brown, "'Little Wing': A Study in Musical Cognition," in John Covach and Graeme M. Boone, eds., *Understanding Rock: Essays in Musical Analysis* (New York and Oxford: Oxford University Press, 1997), 163.

Needlessly obscure prose is always wrong, but precise technical terminology is necessary in musical analysis. When you are writing musical analysis, you are *not* writing for the general reader.

TWO ANALYTICAL EXCERPTS WITH COMMENTARY

In explaining the nature of analysis, strong models will serve better than directives and proscriptions. This excerpt from Leonard Ratner's *Classic Music* discusses the opening of Haydn's Piano Sonata in E-flat Major, Hob. XVI:52:.

Haydn's subtle and eccentric rhetoric asserts itself immediately; the first two measures represent a cadence, a complete statement anchored to a tonic pedal point. This is a powerful gesture, but it is very short, too short for even the briefest of normal periods. To extend it, Haydn uses an echo, itself varied and re-echoed again and again until it gathers momentum to become an agent for continuation in m. 5. The melody arrives at the tonic for the first time at m. 6; we could easily imagine a dominant under the descending parallel thirds in the second half of m. 5, so that the tonic of m. 6 could represent an authentic cadence and the end of the period. But Haydn changes the sense of the tonic twice: first, by underpinning it with C so that a deceptive cadence is suggested; second, by completing the chord with an A♭ so that the harmony becomes IV⁶. At this point, the sixth chord is defined as the carrier of the *stile legato* action, continuing the descent that it began with the first echo. The period ends with a *Tacterstickung* in m. 9, where the tonic serves a double function—arrival and departure. Again the peremptory brevity of the opening figure, always presenting in a two-measure phrase, provides a springboard for contrasting action; this time, the tirata heard in m. 1 becomes a brilliant-style flourish, and the bound style, instead of being the *final* consequence of the echo, enters *early* to rob the cesura of the march figure of its final beat. Throughout the movement, the passage in *stile legato* is treated in a flexible manner; it may enter upon a first, second, third, or fourth beat; it may be 8 to 21 beats in length.[8]

[8]Leonard G. Ratner, *Classic Music* (New York: Schirmer, 1980), 413.

EX. 3.3
Haydn, Sonata in E-flat Major (H.V. XVI:52), I, opening.

Example 3.3 gives the musical excerpt, the opening of the first movement of Haydn's most famous piano sonata. Such concepts as parallel thirds, tonic and dominant, and deceptive and authentic cadences are familiar to anyone who has taken a year of tonal theory, and they need no definition in an analysis of this kind. *Tacterstickung* (a German term meaning "the suppression of a measure"), *stile legato* (not legato articulation, in this case, but "bound style," a reference to the suspensions in the tenor voice, which changes its pitch a quarter-note after the bass and soprano voices do in mm. 6–7), and other terms will not be immediately understood by every music student, but Ratner has explained them earlier in his book. Elements are identified with each other and with fulfilling specific roles: for example, the repeated echo mentioned in the third sentence of the analysis serves both to expand a too-short opening period to a usable length and, once it takes on a life of its own, to serve as an agent for continuation. Ratner's analysis, which here concerns itself primarily with compositional choices in harmony, phrase structure, and surface musical gesture, uses a minimum of jargon yet addresses a range of advanced concepts.

Let us now examine a longer, more detailed excerpt, one that also does not shy away from detail or technical terminology. This excerpt, a discussion of a famous transitional passage from Gershwin's *Rhapsody in Blue,* is taken from Steven Gilbert's book-length analytical study of Gershwin's music.

In short, *Rhapsody in Blue* is not nearly as rhapsodic as it may first seem. Its themes are joined by a multiplicity of motivic relationships. It has a coherent fundamental structure. Where it does appear to meander somewhat, it does so in a controlled way. The processes whereby this control is achieved are central to Gershwin's compositional technique. One is the recursive harmonic progression, which gives the illusion of motion to passages that begin and end in the same place (such as the succession of minor thirds from G to G that is the harmonic basis for the opening of part 2). The other is the transitional passage, a device for which Gershwin, for better or worse, has become well known.

Two such passages make their initial appearance early in part 1. The first, transition 1, begins at R4+6 [Example 3.4] and leads to the A-major entrance of main theme 1 at R4+14, or three bars before R5. Though harmonically static, its upper voices provide considerable interest from the standpoint of both the small and larger dimensions. The initial three measures comprise an ascending sequence supporting the top voice E^2–F^2–G^2, whose vertical cross-sections are each based on the corresponding dominant seventh. The descending portion also begins on an E_7 chord with E^2 in the top voice, whose notes alternate with their upper

EX. 3.4
Gershwin, *Rhapsody in Blue,* Schenkerian graph of transition beginning in m. R4+6.
RHAPSODY IN BLUE™ by GEORGE GERSHWIN © 1924 (Renewed) WB MUSIC CORP.
GERSHWIN® and GEORGE GERSHWIN® are registered trademarks of Gershwin Enterprises.
RHAPSODY IN BLUE™ is a trademark of the George Gershwin Family Trust. All Rights Reserved.

neighbors (diatonic in the first three bars, chromatic in the fourth), creating a whole-tone scale of semitonal dyads. In the fourth measure (whose immediate repetition is not shown), the emphasis shifts from the first to the second note of each dyad, then shifts back at the measure's end.

The larger significance of the upper voices is identical with the underpinning of the entire passage—namely, the dominant of A. The resolution of this dominant provides the clue to the larger melodic progression beamed in Example [3.4]: from E^2 (the starting pitch) to D^1 (the registrally displaced passing seventh, unfolding to $G\sharp$) to $C\sharp^2$. The latter, the resolution of the passing seventh, is absorbed into an inner voice by virtue of the overlapped entrance of main theme 1.[9]

The second of these three paragraphs is not light reading, but I see no way for it to be further clarified or simplified. Gilbert's identification of the melodic implications of the passage (E^2–F^2–G^2 in the first three bars, followed by descending half-step pairs a whole step apart), the harmonic content (dominant seventh chords on the pitches E, F, and G, etc.), and the harmonic implications (it remains on the dominant throughout, despite the suggestion of departure and arrival) is well put,

[9]Steven E. Gilbert, *The Music of Gershwin* (New Haven and London: Yale University Press, 1995), 68–70.

understandable, and above all economical. Even so, it may require several readings to keep track of what is going on—which is not uncommon in specialized writing in any field (think of explanations of mathematical formulae, for example). But notice that a context for this material has been prepared by the first paragraph, which deals with the *Rhapsody* in more general terms, explaining that it is compositionally a lot more tightly constructed than it is usually considered to be, and identifying two compositional aspects that make this so. These two phenomena will be explained in the chosen musical passage (discussed in the second paragraph): recursion (the passage begins and ends on the same chord, E_7, while giving the impression of actually having gone somewhere) and transitionality (meaning that the passage serves as transition from mid-phrase to the next phrase, from cadenza material to the theme that immediately follows, and from rhythmic freedom to rhythmic stability). The reader is thus prepared for the detail immediately following. It then remains for the third paragraph to summarize the importance of the passage by explaining how a particular figure imbedded in the texture (E–D–C♯) relates to the harmony, and to connect the detail to the broader function of the passage.

ORGANIZING ANALYTICAL WRITING

These two analytical excerpts are very different in approach, yet each reaches its goal fairly quickly, with a minimum of jargon. It quickly becomes apparent that there is no single analytical template: there are many persuasive approaches to analysis. In addition to the harmonic, Schenkerian, and set-theory approaches, an analyst might address, for example, rhetorical continuity (one of the earliest analytical approaches), surface musical gestures, scansion and phraseology, or any of a number of stylistic features.

Clear analytical writing depends on a balance between general observations and the individual musical elements that support arguments and illustrate important points. The more general observations are usually stated at the beginning and end of a short paper, or section of a larger study; this enables the author both to prepare the reader to know why a number of small musical features are to be identified and (after) to summarize all the individual observations into a larger, coherent whole—bringing the bigger picture into focus, so to speak. This final analytical excerpt is by the German-born Manfred Bukofzer, one of the clearest and most elegant writers on music in the English language:

> [Giovanni] Gabrieli's later works, composed probably after 1600, breathe a revolutionary spirit affecting all aspects of composition: dissonance treatment, melodic design, rhythmic flow, the attitude toward the words, and the disposition of vocal and instrumental parts. The composer now seized upon the words with a fervor and intensity of affection unprecedented in sacred music. In the motet *Timor et Tremor* [Ex. 3.5] "fear and trembling" is represented in graphic fashion with literally "breathtaking" rests, jagged figures, descending sixths, augmented "false" intervals, and strong dissonances; this music violates nearly all the rules of sixteen-century counterpoint. The beginning is based on a contrast motive characterized by closely juxtaposed notes of very long and very short time

EX. 3.5
Giovanni Gabrieli, *Timor et Temor,* opening.

EX. 3.6
Andrea Gabrieli, *Exaudi Deus,* seconda parte (*Cor Meum Conturbatum Es*), mm. 18–21.

value. The nervous and discontinuous rhythm of these motives is totally at variance with the continuous flow of then old style. The motet *Exaudi Deus* (1565) by Andrea Gabrieli [Ex. 3.6] shows by comparison the restraint with which a true Renaissance composer set the same words.

Later, after presenting illustrative examples from other works, Bukofzer summarizes his argument:

The fervor of word interpretation breathed the mystic and aggressive spirit of the Counter-Reformation which overwhelmed the faithful with gigantic structures, be it in architecture, painting, or music. The nervous sensibility of Gabrieli's novel style inspired only a few kindred Italian composers to continue his path . . . . The true heir to Gabrieli was his greatest German disciple, Schütz, and it is not without symbolic significance that Gabrieli on his deathbed bequeathed his sealing ring to him as if he had a premonition that his pupil would carry the torch that he had lighted.[10]

[10]Manfred Bukofzer, *Music in the Baroque Era: From Monteverdi to Bach* (New York: W. W. Norton, 1947), 22–23, 25. The musical example numbers have been changed, and capitalization of "Renaissance" and "Counter-Reformation" adjusted to reflect current practice.

The basic principles of good analytical organization are apparent from the outset. Bukofzer begins with a general observation about the progressive aspects of Giovanni Gabrieli's newer style of composition, among them the text-music relationship. He illustrates these differences with a setting of the words *Timor et Tremor* (Latin: fear and trembling) as an example, pointing up the newer approaches to rhythms, rests, and linear and vertical writing. After a helpful comparison with a setting of the same text by the composer's uncle Andrea Gabrieli, more examples (not included here) are given, and the section closes with a return to the general—the composer's influence on later generations—and a device beloved of historians, musical and otherwise: the historical anecdote. Bukofzer's analysis-intensive passage proceeds from the general to the specific, and then—when the reader is better prepared to assimilate it—back to the general, where the content and its significance may be elegantly summarized. The generalities are not allowed to rattle on with no specifics to support them, and the specifics are not allowed to accumulate with mind-numbing effect. The balances are confidently struck, and challenging material deftly presented.

A word of caution seems in order here, however. It would be unwise to try to imitate Bukofzer by offering grandiose generalizations about composers' lifelong compositional output or about entire historical periods. Bukofzer was one of the most broadly knowledgeable scholars in the history of the discipline, and his generation, who almost all were reared in the intensive liberal-arts traditions of the European *Gymnasium* and university, relished drawing such connections between music and other arts and cultural phenomena. An elegant and well-organized example such as this teaches a great deal, but aspiring authors should not take Bukofzer's erudition and breadth of vision as an example to be emulated immediately. Play *your* game, as sports commentators always say; organize and craft a coherent structure within the limits of *your* background and research. If the more general parts of your analysis have to do with the single piece you are analyzing and no more, fine. A typical approach to a short analysis paper, for example, is to provide an overview, devote a paragraph or so to each important aspect, and draw the pieces together into a conclusive summary, which might aim at nothing broader than the aspects in which the piece is typical and atypical.

The analyst's business, explaining how a piece works, often consists of pointing out what is noteworthy or interesting about it—how and why this piece works differently from others. Because accounting for *everything* in a piece is both foolhardy and impossible, the analytical approach needs to be clearly established at the beginning of an analysis so that the reader has a clear idea of which questions are going to be asked of a piece. Once the frame of reference is clear, the analysis—of whatever length—can begin to unfold.

The best analyses tread between the subtle and the more apparent. As Jan LaRue put it: "Successful style analysis combines dissection with selection, insight with overview. If we mindlessly proliferate observed details, we may never reach larger understanding."[11] This is only one such balance: analysis also dances between the uniqueness of each artwork and its generic or stylistic relation to other works, between the obscure and what is readily apprehended, and between borrowing from different analytical systems or striking out on one's own. Analysis has the potential to be among the most rigorous and ultimately enlightening activities concerned with studying and writing about music.

[11]Jan LaRue, *Guidelines for Style Analysis* [1970], 2nd ed. (Warren, MI: Harmonie Park Press, 1992), 4.

4

THREE KINDS OF PRACTICAL WRITING

Even now do you think it's much fun for me to be tied to this infernal galley-oar of journalism which affects every aspect of my career? I am so ill that I can hardly hold my pen, yet I am forced to write for my miserable hundred francs ... [1]

—HECTOR BERLIOZ

The writer on musical subjects will be called upon to produce a good deal more than such traditional college assignments as research papers and opinion essays. Several genres of practical writing are found in the musical world: genres that fulfill specific needs, address specific audiences, and sometimes follow specific protocols. (One of these, the concert review, was discussed in Chapter 2.) Command of these kinds of writing enables one:

- to gain experience with the arts community in general, learning what is viable regarding both writing and musical performance
- to become acquainted with the members of the arts community, making friends and profitable connections
- to advocate in effective writing for one's own musical efforts, persuasively communicating the musician's perspective to others who do not share or identify with that perspective
- (occasionally) to make some money

[1]Letter to his son Louis, 14 February 1861, in Humphrey Searle, ed. and trans., *Hector Berlioz: A Selection from His Letters* (New York: Harcourt, Brace, 1966), 169.

To suggest that substantially more money can be made in writing about music than in playing or teaching it would be misleading. As with any endeavor, though, increased experience and skill means that "no money" may become "some money," with further increase depending on skill and situation. The potential benefits of effective writing about music extend well beyond the classroom.

PROGRAM AND LINER NOTES

There are many approaches to writing program notes and liner notes (the printed commentaries that accompany recordings), and every approach is a compromise. Some readers are musically literate but most are probably not, some have performance experience and some do not, some know the repertoire intimately and some do not, and some are passionately devoted to the music being performed and others are not—at all. Given this spectrum, must the annotator take everyone into account? Of course not. Must he or she try to reach the largest cross-section possible? Certainly.

For most readers, program notes that use complex technical vocabulary, feature notated musical examples, and detail formal processes are irrelevant. Listeners who have a solid musical background can recognize themes and their musical adventures without having them notated, and those with less experience will be intimidated or put off by elevated (that is: incomprehensible) academic discussion and analysis, which are rarely of use to the concertgoer. A memorably damning statement about such writing was offered by Claude Debussy's colleague in music criticism, the French writer Colette, who had just attended a performance of a symphony for which the composer's own thematic analysis was provided in the program notes. Colette wrote:

> But then the program did its best to explain . . . How obliging of it! It said, for example, "The rhythmic transformations of figures 4 and 5 lead theme 1 through progressively increasing note values." . . . Then a restatement of the introduction, reexposition, etc. There are, perhaps, people for whom such artifice aids comprehension; it merely makes me feel a fool.[2]

---

[2]As quoted in Claude Debussy, *Debussy on Music*, col. and int. by François Lesure, trans. and ed. by Richard Langham Smith (New York: Alfred A. Knopf, 1977), 128.

It was a gross misjudgment on the composer's part to imagine that a detailed look into his compositional workshop would enhance the enjoyment of the audience at large. Composers do not, as a rule, produce artworks only for the delectation of specialists; far more often they seek to communicate with a broad cross-section of humanity. For the program annotator or the composer to provide an analysis for the first-time listener seems to be a sure way for this kind of direct communication *not* to happen. Ditto for any kind of detailed musical play-by-play, as discussed in Chapter 3; it is the atypical listener (to put it very mildly) who attends a performance with score, flashlight, and outline of the piece so that milestones may be checked off as they are reached. Listening to a new work is certainly a journey, but it is not a road trip.

Another common but counterproductive approach is for the commentary to take a lighthearted approach to the music under discussion. Often predicated on the belief that classical music is valuable in an educational, high-culture, eat-your-spinach-because-it's-good-for-you sort of way, this method targets an imaginary, ultimately disrespected "common person" and seeks to reach him or her on whatever low level the author imagines such a person inhabiting. Writing of this kind is likely to emphasize the prurient or sordid aspects of composers' biographies, to make forced attempts at humor, and to use slang and vernacular inappropriately. The net effect, though unintended, is to insult the reader and trivialize the music, thereby conveying the idea that, since the "entertainment" has to be provided in the commentary, the music is unable to stand on its own. (Radio commentary on classical music stations unfortunately provides ample instances of this approach.) In general, program annotations are a poor venue for humor.

Too often, humor in writing—about music or anything else—falls flat or, worse, demeans its subject. Although a musical work may be hilarious, a joke explained is often a joke neutralized. Musical humor can certainly be identified, or a humorous plot explained quickly and deftly, but unless one seeks to be a musical humorist—and the likes of Victor Borge, Anna Russell, and Peter Schickele (a.k.a. P.D.Q. Bach) are few—a frivolous posture on the part of the annotator does far more harm than good. "Dying is easy; comedy is hard," runs the deathbed observation attributed to various entertainment personalities, and it is a just caution.

The advice so far has been negative, but is not meant to scold. If analysis, play-by-play, and humor are best avoided, what *will* work? Given a general audience ranging from musical novice to experienced listener, what kinds of information will prove to be both helpful and readily understood?

Biographical Background

Biographical information on the composer of a work, judiciously selected and treated, without fixating on the composer's personal life, makes a good starting point. It can both situate a piece at a particular point in the composer's life (overconfident youth? turbulent middle years? magisterial old age?) and connect the work of art with the aspects of being human we all share: living in the world and negotiating its difficulties, having or not having a family, earning recognition and (perhaps) a living, and maintaining a relationship with the wider world of one's peers. Biographical information can establish, for many listeners, a familiar resonance in a largely alien historical realm, thereby opening further doors into that realm.

Cultural Context

We often forget how remote a contemporary listener is from the cultural environment in which much concert music was produced. What did an eighteenth-century listener expect of a sonata, a symphony, an opera, or a sacred work? How do that listener's expectations differ from what we expect today? What aspects of the work in question would listeners have found surprising or astounding? For example, listeners today are so familiar with the technical fireworks of Liszt's piano music, which are now well within the capabilities of many conservatory students and university-level piano majors, that they do not realize that this music was all but unplayable for the vast majority of pianists throughout a good portion of Liszt's lifetime, and that his keyboard talents were therefore sometimes suspected of being supernatural. Finding a way to relate each piece to its own world helps the audience to see it as something other than a relic, and that is always more interesting to the listener than "Here is [yet] one more virtuosic piece by that master of the violin, Fritz Kreisler . . . "

Style and Affect

It is a good idea for the annotator to say a word or two about style and mood. A listener who knows a work will not be offended by an intelligent reminder of something already understood, and it will not hurt for another listener, one perhaps more familiar with such popular classical works as Pachelbel's D major canon and Tchaikovsky's suite from the

Nutcracker ballet, to be made aware that the knotty dissonances of a Bartók string quartet or the ironic, painful emotional content of a Shostakovich symphony are about to be heard. But finer points of musical style are best left alone, in consideration of the needs and experience of the average audience member. A good rule of thumb is for the commentary to provide, in addition to whatever biographical and historical context the annotator deems helpful, one or at most a very few things to listen for. More is probably too much for the listener to use.

Writing for the general, symphony-attending public is a balancing act. On the one hand, it is dangerous to assume that the audience has any musical training at all; readers unfamiliar with the annotator's terms or concepts may feel insulted or alienated. On the other hand, any art music (including Western concert music) is an acquired taste, and those who are interested in it probably have a strong educational background and cultural awareness—and they will be put off by too chatty a tone or too simplistic a discussion. The difficulty in finding an appropriate tone lies in walking the line between a high level of education and a merely rudimentary understanding of music.

One elegant solution to this problem is seen in the following discussion of an instrumental canzona by Giovanni Gabrieli, written by Scott Warfield for a performance by the North Carolina Symphony.

Giovanni Gabrieli (b. c. 1554–7; d. 1612)

Canzon septimi toni No. 2

Venice, at the end of the Renaissance, was one of the most glorious cities in Europe. As the primary port of entry for goods arriving from the East, the city prospered on the tariffs imposed on that cargo. Moreover, Venice was a quasi-democracy run by elected officials, and thus patronage for the arts came primarily from civic coffers or from the temporal leaders' own funds, rather than from royalty. Public spectacles, like the famous "Wedding with the Sea" ceremony, were frequent, and musical instruments—notably the six silver trumpets that symbolized the power and prestige of the Doge—were a common sight in the central piazza before the great Church of St. Mark's.

Musical instruments were also a regular part of the services inside that church long before instrumental music had become a common feature of Baroque sacred music in the seventeenth century. In 1568, Girolamo Dalla Casa and his two brothers, performers on the cornetto and other wind instruments, were appointed as the first permanent instrumentalists in the cappella of St. Mark's. Extra players were also frequently hired, and by the end of the century, ensembles of as many as twenty instrumentalists could be heard on certain feast days, with the exceptional size of St. Mark's encouraging the disposition of performers in small groups on either side of the nave.

This technique of *cori spezzati* (literally, "broken choirs") found its greatest exponent in Giovanni Gabrieli, organist at St. Mark's from about 1584 until his death. Giovanni had doubtless learned this technique from his uncle, Andrea Gabrieli, who likewise had served St. Mark's as its organist. Still, it was probably Giovanni Bassano, Dalla Casa's successor as leader of the church's instrumentalists, who made an even greater impact on G. Gabrieli's instrumental works. Bassano was a virtuoso on the cornetto (a wooden instrument with finger holes that was nevertheless played with the technique of vibrating lips common to all modern brass instruments), who published one of the first treatises on how to ornament and embellish simple melodies with quicker moving "diminutions" of the line.

Giovanni Gabrieli's instrumental canzonas are thus quite remarkable in an age that barely acknowledged the existence of musical instruments. Instead of the vocal styles that normally served as models for early instrumental works, Gabrieli's canzonas are filled with purely instrumental effects—repeated notes, dance rhythms, sequences with virtuosic ornamentation, and echo effects—that singers generally could not perform. Gabrieli also met the challenge of organizing his musical ideas without a text. Most of his canzonas are built out of a series of discrete sections, each featuring a single melodic, harmonic or rhythmic idea, and usually one or more of these reappears somewhere in the work. In the Canzon septimi toni No. 2, the opening section and its immediate continuation return at the end of the work just before a brief coda. "Septimi toni" ("seventh tone") of the title refers to the seventh church mode—notes equivalent to G to G on the white keys of a piano—of medieval and Renaissance music theory. Nevertheless, Gabrieli's use of simple triadic harmonies gives his work an extremely modern sound for its time.

Note that the treatment of the canzona itself ("canzon" is a variant spelling the composer used for the title of the work, hence the orthographic disparity) is confined to the final paragraph, which summarizes characteristics of all such pieces (repeated notes, dance rhythms, echo effects, and virtuosic ornamentation), gives a definition of the "seventh tone" mentioned in the title, and suggests one formal feature to listen for (the return of the opening material near the end of the work). This information provides more than enough for the untrained audience members to listen for: typical characteristics and a specific, important sound event. The bulk of the program annotation gives a contextual picture of the Venetian economic and cultural environment that produced such pieces, including the atypically important role played by instrumental music. It is true that a certain educational level on the part of the audience is presumed, but inordinate demands have not been made of its musical preparation. The reader is informed—taught—not insulted or excluded.

One ever-present consideration in program-note writing is the problem of length. This is not the place for a full discussion of the realities of program booklets, layout, and advertising space, save to warn that plenty of wild cards are involved in any kind of publishing and it is often the author who must do the accommodating. The nature of the evening's program will determine a good deal of what you can and cannot write about it. For an entire program made up of one piece, such as a major work for chorus, soloists, and orchestra, you can afford to address the genesis of the work, the text, the style, the historical circumstances, and even perhaps something specific about each movement. An evening of favorite opera arias, though, may not leave you with room for much more than the titles of the numbers to be sung. Of course, most programs lie in between, so some flexibility is often helpful and even necessary.

The following note for a concerto by Tomaso Albinoni provides an example of a kind of reverse pyramid structure (traditional pyramid structure will be discussed below in connection with writing press releases), in which the third of the three paragraphs has the most specific information, the second paragraph has some general biographical background on the composer, and the first addresses a piece commonly (but wrongly) associated with the composer that might be familiar to listeners. The paragraphs are all self-standing, and if the first and even the second must be deleted for reasons of space, the third provides adequate preparation for a listener to hear the work.

Tomaso Albinoni (1671–1751)

Concerto for Two Oboes and Strings in C Major, op. 9 no. 9

Tomaso Albinoni is best known to audiences for the famous *Adagio*, a perennial Baroque favorite almost as well known as Pachelbel's *Canon in D* and Handel's *Music for the Royal Fireworks*. This is one of music history's great jokes, because the *Adagio* is not by Albinoni at all, but rather is the product of one Remo Giazotto, an Italian musicologist and Albinoni scholar who claimed that the bassline and some melodic ideas originated with a trio sonata fragment rescued from the ruins of Dresden in the immediate aftermath of WWII. The fragment itself seems, unsurprisingly, not to be traceable, and what is particularly ironic is that the sentimentality and excess of the *Adagio* are completely at odds with the clarity and vigor of Albinoni's instrumental style.

Albinoni was one of the earliest composers to survive without a court or church position. The eldest son of a wealthy paper merchant, he devoted himself at an early stage to singing and violin-playing, and later to composition. In fact, it is revealing that when his father died in 1709, Tomaso's customary rights of inheritance were bypassed, and the business passed to his two younger brothers, although he was guaranteed a third of the income. That he was explicitly forbidden involvement with the business suggests both a wholehearted devotion to music and perhaps also a certain incompetence in financial and practical matters—a frequent and time-honored pairing of personality traits. After 1721, when income from the family business dried up as a result of a lawsuit by one of his father's creditors, he was able to support himself through his singing-school and compositions.

The opus 9 concertos were published in 1722, and represent Albinoni's instrumental writing at its most assured and confident. The first movement of no. 9 is cast in traditional *concerto grosso* format, which is to say that statements by the full ensemble, which begin with an easily-recognized melodic "motto," alternate with more extended passages for the soloists. The oboes are used almost exclusively as a team, playing together (in parallel thirds, mostly) rather than trading virtuosic solos, and seem to be enjoying the sheer beauty of sound as much as the listeners are. The second movement focuses on the oboe's yearning and pleading qualities; in the best Baroque tradition, a powerful effect is produced by elegant, understated writing. The final movement returns to Albinoni's trademark rhythmic liveliness and dancelike character to bring the concerto to a joyful close. One can't help feeling that such a pleasing and listenable work has a legitimate place on "Baroque Favorites" CDs, and would both appeal to a wide audience and earn the composer fame for a piece he had actually written.

Proceeding through a concert program with treatments of individual pieces, which is the usual strategy, is not necessarily the most interesting one. A more creative approach might be to first address the concert program as a whole, discussing whatever stylistic, cultural, or historical background is common to the repertoire, and then go on to examine each work individually. Imagine a very typical program of concert overture, concerto, and symphony; this might be a good time for a novice's introduction to sonata-allegro form, which then allows each piece performed to be related to the form in one or another clear ways. If the pieces are all by one composer, a general essay on the composer followed by short discussions of the pieces might serve very nicely. Or perhaps the works on the program share some kind of association with dance, or with popular musical forms and styles, or their national origin. For the program annotator to begin with the general and move on to the specific is effective, and especially creative when the unifying idea was not involved in the choice of pieces—when, in other words, it is the annotator who first notices the unifying feature. Such an approach ties the entire program into a nice package for the listener, and might enable more experienced audience members to hear pieces in a new way.

The annotator thus walks several tightropes: between what the listener probably already knows and what may be entirely new; between what is musically obvious and what may require more listener concentration to pick up; and—most difficult of all—between the inappropriate extreme (what is either simple-minded or hopelessly obscure) on the one hand and that golden area of new material or concepts that listeners are prepared to learn on the other. Not to be forgotten, of course, are the tightropes associated with space in the program book and deadlines for submission! Each audience presents a different challenge, as does each new concert program, and in the end the consistent production of program notes is one of the very best ways to learn a good deal about both music and writing about it.

SUMMARIES AND ABSTRACTS

Summaries and abstracts represent two different solutions to a frequently misunderstood problem. The problem lies in rendering in a few words (exactly how few will vary with the situation) the essence of a large piece of writing, such as a scholarly article, a master's thesis, or a doctoral dissertation. Since the entire content cannot be retained, decisions regarding what to include and omit must be made at the beginning. The preference for either summary or abstract will depend on the use for which it is intended.

The Summary

A formal *summary* explains what the author was doing in a particular piece of writing and what results were shown or conclusions drawn. Summaries emphasize that the article in question is being described by a third party, so constructions like "the author states" and "this study shows" may occasionally be used. (Although some forbid the use of such phrases, I consider it permissible. The emphasis or de-emphasis of the author's role is one of the key differences between summaries and abstracts; summaries *stress* the author's role and responsibility, and abstracts do not.) Another element specific to summaries is that more weight is placed on the conclusions: what was shown, what came to be proven, what resulted. Summaries are often used in annotated bibliographies and the literature review sections of theses and dissertations, two kinds of documents in which a variety of sources are examined and evaluated, so the emphasis on results and conclusions is appropriate.

The following article summary and abstract pertain to the research paper "Gershwin's French Connection" by Amie Margoles (the paper itself appears in Chapter 7 of this book). Commentary will follow each.

Margoles's paper provides a French context for Gershwin's music, especially the tone poem *An American in Paris*. The biographical and anecdotal background is presented first, and includes the well-known anecdotes of Gershwin's use of actual

French taxi horns and his rebuffs from Maurice Ravel and Nadia
Boulanger regarding composition lessons. The author then outlines
the various French musical influences on the work, and concludes
that the resultant combination of all these French elements with the
American popular musics Gershwin knew so well resulted in a
wholly American piece clearly based upon and inspired by French
musical trends.

The primary focus here is the conclusion: *An American in Paris* is neither purely French nor purely American, and this is because the American
composer had a great interest in French music and visited France. This
summary would be appropriate for use in an annotated bibliography; the
reader would get an idea of both the main point of the article and the related issues the author addresses, but without the arguments, the specifics,
and so on. For the limited purposes of a summary, this is sufficient.

The Abstract

A formal *abstract* is a purely academic kind of writing, a presentation of
the article itself in miniature, and it is proportionally similar to the original: introduction, premises, evidence, discussion, conclusions. Unlike
summaries, abstracts place more emphasis on methodology, argument,
and proof; it is not just the conclusions that are important, in other words,
but rather how the author arrives at them. In scholarly publications,
abstracts often accompany the articles on which they are based, and they
also appear in collections and standard bibliographic databases (such as
RILM Abstracts of Musical Literature).

A good abstract enables a reader—perhaps a student or scholar who
needs to be aware of developments in a particular field but does not have
the leisure to read every article in detail—to get a clear idea of the totality of an article: methodology and thought process in addition to conclusions. The reader finds more information in a strong abstract than in a
summary because it addresses not only the destination but the nature of
the journey, the steps taken to arrive at the conclusions.

Another important difference between abstracts and summaries is
that summaries stress the role of the author in the writing ("Margoles's
paper provides" and "the author then outlines"). Abstracts, however,
should be written from (so to speak) inside the article. The person

producing the abstract acts as author of the article (and articles are often abstracted by their authors): stating the problem, presenting evidence, pointing to the conclusions—all in a very few words—without suggesting that another piece of writing is being discussed. It is as if the entire piece is freeze-dried into its most condensed form, with all essential elements intact.

Here is an abstract of the Margoles paper:

George Gershwin's 1923 and 1928 trips to Paris were revelatory experiences for him. Prodigiously gifted musically but lacking in both formal education and wider cultural experience, he reacted to all Parisian stimuli—the wealthy and cultured individuals he met, the high-end restaurants and cabarets, the street scenes—with excitement and delight. No less attractive to him was the French music scene, with which he concerned himself particularly on the second visit: having already met Ravel back in New York, he met the famed teacher Nadia Boulanger and the composers Milhaud, Poulenc, and Stravinsky, among others. Before leaving Paris, Gershwin acquired scores of the complete works of Debussy, whose musical language (like that of the composers of Les Six) is reflected in the tone poem *An American in Paris*, as are (in Gershwin's own words) the "various street noises" and the "French atmosphere." While his works do use such French elements as parallel chords, pentatonic arpeggios, and Stravinskian changing meters, it is clear that French music had interested him long before he visited, and that in any case French musical devices had already become part of the vocabulary of American art music.

The paper itself proceeds from Gershwin's first visit to Paris and enchantment with the city, to his more focused 1928 visit and the musical personalities he met, to the more specific musical elements he associated with France, to their presence in *An American in Paris* and other works, to the conclusion about the happy amalgam of French and American musics. The abstract seeks to follow precisely this train of thought, neither emphasizing one aspect more than the author does nor trying to include every last detail and making every last distinction. As a miniaturization of the article, it must be less casual than a summary but is useful in more ways.

Summaries and abstracts are thus two discrete but often confused forms. Unfortunately, what are in fact summaries are often mislabeled as abstracts (the opposite mistake is not made nearly as often). But writing them is an extremely valuable exercise: reducing another author's article to a miniature requires a familiarity with and understanding of the original article or work that even two or three close readings will not yield. For an article central to your research project or field, an article you absolutely have to know, the abstracting process is invaluable.

THE PRESS RELEASE

The press release, properly done, demands as little creativity as possible. (I distinguish between actual press releases and press announcements that inflate themselves by inappropriately incorporating advertising copy and puff material. There is no need to discuss the latter variety, which is writing intended to mislead.) The function of a press release is to publicize an upcoming event, and it should be as effective as possible. The difficulty lies in the fact that press releases can be used in different ways. A press release provides basic information that can be presented in various formats: as published listings of events, as announcements and fliers, or as a Public Service Announcement to be read aloud on a local radio station. For such uses, only basic information is appropriate: who, what, when, where, how much. In as concise a fashion as possible, people need to be told who is playing the concert, what kind of concert it is, when and where people should show up for it, how much money they will need for tickets, and how they can get further information. Traditionally, the last two items, ticket prices and an information number, close the press release.

This is all the hard information that is necessary. But because newspapers sometimes print press releases verbatim as mini-articles, more is required when writing one. Since space is a paramount concern in newspaper writing, the author of a press release must use what is called "pyramid form," where the absolutely essential material occurs at the beginning, and what follows is helpful but less and less necessary. (The name derives from the idea that chunks of the press release may have to be deleted, and this form makes the editing process unproblematic—when the bottom chunk is cut off, the "pyramid" still stands; it is simply smaller.)

Here is an example, written by Susan Nelson, the Director of Arts Information at the University of Northern Colorado:

November 19, 1993

FOR MORE INFORMATION CONTACT:

Susan Nelson, 123-4567

The University of Northern Colorado's Concert Band, Symphonic Band, and Wind Ensemble will perform at 8 p.m. on Tuesday, November 23, at Foundation Hall, 1516 Eighth Avenue.

Under the direction of Dr. Kenneth Singleton and Dr. Richard Mayne, the ensembles will present a wide variety of band literature. The UNC bands have received national and international recognition, with ensembles having been invited to perform at numerous state and national conventions, and having produced a series of important wind recordings and publications.

The performance is open to the public without charge.

For more information, please contact the UNC Bands Office at 345-6789.

The final two sentences about cost and contact information are *not* optional; in this example the base of the pyramid must remain. In the computer age, deleting a block from the middle of a press release is no more complex than cutting off the end. But note the general adherence to a pyramid approach: what is most important about the event is stated in the first brief paragraph. For the newspaper, and for others that might need more and want to quote directly, the names of the directors and comments on the repertoire and the reputation of the bands (all on an appropriate, publicity-based level) are provided.

Another possibility is to include quotations from a participant in the release, and to provide more information. In the following four-paragraph example, the structure is a true pyramid: each succeeding paragraph is of slightly less importance, and the release could function in one-, two-, or three-paragraph versions. Information may easily be gleaned from it for radio announcements, and the whole still works fine as a newspaper article.

November 20, 1990

FOR FURTHER INFORMATION CONTACT:

Susan Nelson, 123-4567

An evening of dance will be presented by the University of Northern Colorado Dance Department at 7:30 p.m. Tuesday, December 4, in Gunter Hall, room 107, 10th Avenue and Cranford Place, Greeley.

An informal showcase, the Gunter Hall performances will feature the department's Dance Tour Troupe and several of the dance classes. Tickets cost $2 apiece, with proceeds to benefit the UNC Dance Scholarship Fund. For tickets and additional information, call the dance department, 234-5678.

"The evening is presented as an opportunity for members of the Beginning Jazz and Modern Dance, as well as the Intermediate Jazz, Ballet, and Modern Dance classes, to show off what they've learned," said Carolyn Genoff Campbell, head of the Dance Tour Troupe. "It's a way for class members to perform for roommates, friends and parents, and apply what they've learned to a performance situation."

The evening will also include a performance by the department's Dance Tour Troupe, 12 students who choreograph their own works under the supervision of [the Director] and perform at schools throughout Colorado. Formed in 1977, the troupe presents a variety of dance styles, including jazz, modern, lyrical, and primitive, to audiences of all ages.

The central idea with press releases, abstracts, summaries, and other kinds of "occasional" writing such as publicity puff pieces is that the author's personality, mastery of the language, and unique voice *need to be well in the background*. (This is less true for program or liner notes.) Practical writing has specific purposes, and it must satisfy these purposes in order to provide readers what they need. There is little romance here!

But compare this kind of writing with other musical activity. The greatest musical virtuosi, the interpreters with the most profound command of their instruments, have spent long hours practicing technical exercises. Similarly, the greatest composers, historically, spent much of their training not only copying over other composers' works but producing highly structured and formulaic exercises in counterpoint and harmony. So it is with all kinds of practical writing: the discipline is irreplaceable, much experience may be gained, and a good deal about the craft of writing may be learned from such clearly defined tasks.

5

BELIEFS INTO WORDS: OPINION AND THE WRITING OF AN EFFECTIVE ESSAY

Logic! Good gracious! What rubbish! How can I tell what I think till I see what I say?[1]

—E. M. FORSTER, *ASPECTS OF THE NOVEL*

Producing an essay that persuades someone to your way of thinking, or at least raises doubts in the mind of a reader holding the opposite position, is a great challenge. As with other genres, the author has to strike balances: between an inflammatory tone and an inoffensively bland one, between unsupported raving and an argument smothered in supporting data and other minutiae. Command of the essay form, once achieved, will benefit virtually every other genre of writing; research papers, reviews, and program notes are shaped by a writer's persuasiveness in the same way that essays invariably benefit from the author's command of research method, listening skills, and quality of musical understanding. So, although essays on musical subjects are far more common inside the

---

[1]E. M. Forster, in "The Plot," the fifth chapter of *Aspects of the Novel* (1927). This comment is offered as the riposte of "that old lady in the anecdote who was accused by her nieces of being illogical."

university environment than outside it, the skills learned in essay preparation will benefit a lifetime of writing. As the practical musician isolates a technical or interpretive problem to solve through focused effort, so the author seeks to master persuasion by writing essays.

PRESENTATION AND TONE

Organization

In an essay, as with concert reviews and program notes (discussed in Chapters 2 and 4, respectively), decisions regarding organization need to be made before the writing begins. This does *not* mean that these decisions, once made, are irrevocable; rather, it means that arguments are best laid out within a broader framework. The framework may well be changed later, and such a change will likely necessitate adjustments in the writing. But proceeding toward completion with the guidance of a well-considered outline (more on outlines below) is far more effective than beginning to write with a blank screen or a blank piece of paper. Since the central goal of an essay is persuasion, the author has to consider much more than evidence and the intrinsic merit of the position to be defended. Organization and presentation require care.

Thoughts must proceed in a logical sequence; transitions must be clear, convincing, and *not* jarring; and conclusions must follow naturally, as the obvious and unavoidable results of the ideas presented. This formula is especially important when your point is speculative or controversial. The more radical the idea, the more ironclad the presentation must be, since the resistance it must overcome will be greater.

Confrontational Writing

Writers, professional as well as undergraduate, often assume that a confrontational approach results in vigorous, persuasive writing. Confrontational writing implies, by its very nature, that if an idea is worth holding, all other ideas ought to be disparaged, even with hostility and resentment, and that those who hold them are mentally and morally suspect. Politically influenced writing sometimes inspires this kind of excess; authors flatter themselves in believing that stakes are much higher than with "mere" academic or musical issues. Locating one's musical or critical position within Inexorable Historical Forces or the Great Moral Balance lends, not surprisingly, a sense of self-righteousness and desperation to the discussion. In all cases, we must remember that however firmly we hold a position, we seek to inform and persuade, not harangue and incite.

Because confrontational writing is both uncivil and counterproductive, it is wrong, as the following examples will illustrate. (Since the influence of political issues is not a requirement for such writing, I deliberately avoid using that kind of example so as to leave questions of ideological loyalty and political position out of the discussion altogether.) Consider, instead, this final portion of the last paragraph of Harold Truscott's scholarly introduction to an edition of the piano sonatas of Johann Nepomuk Hummel (1778–1837), a slightly younger contemporary of Beethoven and a student of Mozart and Muzio Clementi. The introduction was primarily devoted to Hummel's biography, his musical compositions, and matters of style, interpretation, and performance practices relevant to the study of his music. Until its closing section it is completely appropriate—a helpful guide to the music it introduces. At the end, Truscott suggests that the best technical preparation for studying Hummel's sonatas may be the exercises in Clementi's *Gradus ad Parnassum.* He then (inexplicably) concludes:

> By the time this work [*Gradus*] has been mastered, the pianist will be ready to tackle any type of piano technique, excluding those techniques (if that is the word) known as avant-garde. For plucking piano strings, sawing off piano legs or in other ways destroying the instrument, sitting in silence watching the piano warily in case it bites, and hitting the keyboard or producing *glissandi* with one's knuckles, forearms, nose or teeth, with the further aid of French chalk—or using what is called a "prepared" piano, which means that it is prepared for use as anything but a musical instrument—for these things Clementi did not provide. Grimaldi, or Grock, or some other such artist, I should say[,] would have been best equipped to produce a text-book or "method" on such matters. But Hummel's sonatas do not require these techniques. In addition to the physical techniques covered by Clementi's *Gradus*, they do require something else also covered by the Clementi work, but absent from the territory of avant-garde techniques, and that is musicianship.[2]

Mr. Truscott is welcome to his opinion about prepared pianos, nontraditional ways of playing traditional instruments (more accurately called

---

[2]Harold Truscott, Foreword to Johann Nepomuk Hummel, *Complete Piano Sonatas* (London: Musica Rara, 1974), ix.

"extended techniques"), the relevance of famous English clowns Grimaldi and Grock to such approaches to performance, John Cage's *4'33"* (though it remains unnamed, there is a specific dig about this piece), and anything else. Nonetheless, he is not welcome to rant, and his inclusion of such a snide, off-topic closing section in a discussion of Hummel's piano sonatas goes well beyond authorial right and propriety. This passage may first strike readers as amusing, particularly if we are resistant to most piano music of the twentieth century (a position that may well change with more experience), but on sober reflection we wonder why the passage is there, and why we are being confronted with a completely irrelevant matter.

Worse yet is the opening of Henry Pleasants's 1955 book *The Agony of Modern Music:*

> Serious Music is a dead art.
>
> The vein which for three hundred years offered a seemingly inexhaustible yield of beautiful music has run out. What we know as modern music is the noise made by deluded spectators picking through the slagpile.[3]

This passage is consciously insulting. It serves notice that the book's entire premise is the Golden Age Fallacy: everything is terrible in these decadent times, and it was all much better before (whenever the arbitrary "before" might have been—the author's 1655 starting point excludes the entire Renaissance and early Baroque repertoires, for whatever reason). The rhetoric, moreover, is dishonest: Pleasants's aesthetic contrast, "beautiful" music with "the noise made by deluded spectators," masks the implied moral contrast: seriousness vs. the slagpile, value vs. accumulated waste. His tone is indefensible, and for an attentive reader it undermines his position through its very shrillness. When an author yells or sneers rather than presents an idea for consideration with at least a modicum of civility, when a statement seems more suited to a bumper sticker than a paper, article, or book, then it badly needs to be revised or thrown out.

I do not mean to imply that there is no merit in passionately held positions *per se,* political or otherwise, or that positions are not worth defending with conviction. Positions are, ideally, the products of our opinions, beliefs, and ultimately our values, and a well-reasoned and

---

[3]Henry Pleasants, *The Agony of Modern Music* (New York: Simon and Schuster, 1955), 3.

firmly held position says a great deal about the person holding it. But strength of position or belief is not the same thing as stridency of rhetoric. Writing that reflects solid convictions and clear thinking throughout, carefully crafted writing in which clear attention has been devoted to presentation, elegance, and rhetorical restraint, will always be more powerful and persuasive than undisciplined venting.

Stylistic Excess

Stylistic excess consists of attempts to fortify an argument (in the same way that breakfast cereals of dubious nutritional value are fortified with added vitamins and nutrients) with superlatives, overly colorful adjectives, or exaggerated wording. Compare the following two passages:

> M. Chopin is . . . a dealer in the most absurd and hyperbolical extravagances. . . . The entire works of Chopin present a motley surface of ranting hyperbole and excruciating cacophony. . . . There is an excuse at present for Chopin's delinquencies: he is entrammelled in the enthralling bonds of that arch-enchantress, George Sand, celebrated equally for the number and excellence of her romances and her lovers.[4]

and

> The music of Frédéric Chopin has shown a troubling predisposition for overstatement and dissonance, characteristics also seen in the novels of George Sand, with whom Chopin has shared his life for some years.

The difference in content is minimal; I drafted the second passage in an attempt to reword the first (taken from a nineteenth-century music review) as calmly as possible. The original dulls the reader's senses with its procession of highly charged, multisyllabic words. There is also a subtly confrontational (not to say moralizing) undercurrent: to oppose the author's evaluation would be to stand up and defend "ranting hyperbole and excruciating cacophony." None of it is necessary, and it is noteworthy that no actual proof is offered. Of course, stylistic excesses do not have to be insult-laden; they can be flowery, faux-literary effusions, or

---

[4]Anonymous review in the *Musical World* (London), 28 October 1841, quoted in Nicholas Slonimsky, *Lexicon of Musical Invective* [1953] (London and Seattle: University of Washington Press, 1978), 84.

impenetrable pseudo-intellectualism. Regardless of the author's perspective, though, writing of this kind proclaims the fundamental weakness of the argument, and the author's insecurity and defensiveness in putting it forth.

THE WRITING PROCESS: FROM OUTLINE TO FINAL DRAFT

Essay writing, as stated above, needs to take place within the framework of a plan. This plan, the outline, is a requirement for virtually all writing, and arranging the parts of the outline in the most effective order is not a job to be rushed. A good outline facilitates prose writing in all ways: it ensures that a project is logically thought through at the outset, it provides the structural roadmap by which the writing can proceed, and it can serve as a lifeline to authors who get lost in their own prose, arguments, subject matter, or voluminous notes. (This includes all of us, at one time or another.) Of course, outlines are not carved in stone; if the writing process comes to suggest a better way of organizing the paper, both outline and paper may be changed. But a well-considered and carefully crafted outline is the surest guide to a successfully organized and workable first draft, and it will ultimately save a great deal of work.

Let us examine a short essay by Jessica Mosier, an undergraduate cello student at the time it was written, and use it to illustrate the outlining process. She presents a defense of the Suzuki method of instrumental music pedagogy, based on her personal experience as a Suzuki piano and cello pupil. (Remember, our business is to examine this essay's organization and style; its appearance here is neither an endorsement of one method of instrumental instruction nor an implicit critique of any other method.)

Benefits of the Suzuki Method

by Jessica Mosier

The Suzuki method of learning to play an instrument is surrounded by controversy. Some people say that it is not a good way to learn to play an instrument. I disagree; I began learning the Suzuki method of piano at age six, and it was one of the best experiences I ever had. It taught me skills that I use today, not only in playing music, but also in other areas of my life.

One of these skills is the ability to listen. Along with the required Suzuki books, I was required to purchase tapes of the music being played. I listened to these tapes at every opportunity. Consequently, I knew the notes to the pieces before I even began to play them on the piano. After I knew the notes, it was just a matter of learning where to put my fingers. Even now, I listen to recordings of my repertoire before I begin playing it. I believe this gives me a head start in learning a piece because I know what it is supposed to sound like. This ability to listen also helps me today, because I have noticed that I pay closer attention in class than my peers who perhaps did not learn the Suzuki method. Even as a young child, I was trained to stop what I was doing and listen to the teacher giving directions. I feel that this training has helped me achieve higher grades because I always knew what was going on.

Another benefit of the Suzuki method is the belief that the parent is an important part of teaching the child. I began playing Suzuki cello at age nine, and my mother sat in on my lessons and took notes, just as she did when I took Suzuki piano. When it was time to practice at home, she was there with me to be sure that I practiced correctly. Since she had been at the lessons, she knew what to reinforce, and what to improve. She was also there to give me encouragement when I needed it most. I believe that this portion of the Suzuki method greatly promotes a nurturing family environment, which is something that is seriously lacking in our society today.

Still another skill I learned from the Suzuki method is the ability to concentrate. I believe that concentration is extremely important, not only in music, but also in other areas. When I practice in the university practice rooms, I find that I am able to tune out peripheral noise, and concentrate on my playing. Deep concentration such as this comes in very handy when I play recitals; I am able to forget that anyone else is in the room, aside from my accompanist. This ability to concentrate also helps me greatly when I take tests. I can tune out the noise of other people, and think only about the task at hand. As a result, I am not distracted by others' moving around while I am still taking the test.

Overall, I think that the Suzuki method is a very good way to learn an instrument because students learn not only music, but also skills that they will carry with them their whole lives.

Ms. Mosier's essay illustrates several effective strategies for persuasive writing. Her organization is clear: the opening paragraph explains the issue she intends to discuss, each of the next three paragraphs provides one supporting argument plus commentary and discussion, and the last paragraph is a single summarizing sentence. This organization, which reflects forethought, is the direct result of the outlining process. We can imagine that her first scrawled, brainstormed outline (or simple list of ideas) might have looked something like this:

Suzuki Method

1. Suzuki method—how it worked for me
2. Listening skills
3. Mom's role
4. Learning to concentrate
5. Conclusions

A rereading of this list suggests that while it is helpful, one cannot very well start writing from something so general. Accordingly, we can further imagine Ms. Mosier sitting down with her list and producing a second, fleshed-out version of the outline that could have looked something like the following.

I. Premise: Suzuki method as effective method of instrumental instruction
   A. Controversy about it
   B. List of objections

    C. My experience

    D. Other life skills taught

  II. Listening skills

    A. Required tapes

      1. Knowing tunes before learning to play or read

      2. Repetition and reinforcement

    B. Benefits in learning repertoire today—hearing it first

    C. Benefits in class, listening to teachers, higher grades, etc.

  III. Mom's role

    A. Sat in on lessons, as per method, like a second teacher

      1. Could help me practice, reinforce corrections, and work on areas needing improvement

      2. Could offer encouragement and support when needed— all week, not just at lesson

    B. Strengthens parent-child bond in general—Much needed in families today, etc.

  IV. Ability to concentrate

    A. Musical advantages

      1. Tuning out outside noise in practice rooms

      2. Concentrating during performance, not getting thrown by extraneous noise or movement

    B. Other advantages

      1. Test-taking—others' restlessness not bothering me

  V. Conclusions (Whatever!)

From this outline, she could certainly begin to write, crafting a sentence or two for each idea, with the outline functioning as scaffolding. The result is a solid organizational structure, with clear, logical progress from initial idea to conclusions.

Notice also the advantage of using the writing process to reconsider each point in the outline, allowing for the possibility of changing one's mind. For example, item I.B, the list of others' objections to the method advocated, did not make it from the outline into the essay. Here it is the right decision, as there are plenty of positive arguments for the Suzuki method, and since this is primarily a personal paper the more controversial aspects of this method are not raised and don't particularly need to be addressed. (I refer to the postponement of music literacy and the greater dependence on the quality of the teacher than in traditional methods; to introduce the pros and cons would have required a much longer paper.) This does raise, however, an important ethical question: to what extent should the author of a work of opinion offer counterarguments to his or her own position? I consider it the intellectual and moral strength of people who see the world as complex and contradictory that they need to consider different points of view. It follows that a fair essay will often devote some attention to counterarguments to the advocated position, with respectful paraphrase and principled rebuttal of the contrary position. A certain amount depends on the issue, certainly; in a paper that calls for more respect for and understanding of Praise Music, for example, responding to an opposing position like "Praise Music is simply the bland, denatured derivative of other styles such as country and pop-rock" would simply be a waste of time and space, and in an essay time and space are at a premium. (What would the response be—"It is *not!*"?) Polemical battles of that sort have to be weighed carefully.

The sad fact remains that the majority of the human race is far more comfortable with binary models: us vs. them, good vs. bad, righteous vs. damnable. This mental laziness is not limited to matters of religion, political affiliation, or form of government; in the musical realm, it can be seen in how much respect some young people show for each others' differing musical tastes, for example, or how advocates or critics of classical music characterize those taking differing positions. A writer of this two-dimensional mindset (think of the Pleasants example given earlier) misrepresents and satirizes an opposing viewpoint in order to provoke contempt and derision. Distorting or excluding a counterargument is imagined to be a rhetorical benefit—people aren't likely to have sympathy for something so poorly represented—but paradoxically, it is not (for thinking people, at least). The writer who does not give fair treatment to a responsible opposing opinion fears it, and moreover lacks confidence in his or her own position. Again, however, this does depend on the topic; for Ms. Mosier to have tried to fairly represent and respond to a position like "Forget family involvement; it's the kid's music lesson, so don't bother the parent" would have been counterproductive. As a general rule, though, the essayist has a moral and intellectual responsibility to consider and treat with respect—within logistical limits—opposing viewpoints.

One effective tactic the author did use was to link the musical advantages of the method to benefits enjoyed in nonmusical life. A paper aimed at musicians (or a music professor) thus connects its issues to the wider world and shows how a method of musical instruction also develops nonmusical skills. Listening and concentration skills in all areas are developed, the parent becomes a second Suzuki teacher, and the commitment of family members to each other is reinforced. (Ms. Mosier assumes that the reader will agree that this is a good thing, and for the majority of readers this is a safe assumption.) In this way the author strengthens her musical point by relating it to a far bigger picture. Since nonmusical benefits make up a good part of the Suzuki philosophy and tradition, this might seem (to those familiar with the Suzuki method) a relatively obvious card to play, but one aspect of good essay writing consists of perceiving such opportunities and capitalizing on them, placing one's material and reasoning in the most advantageous light.

To improve the essay further, Ms. Mosier might have expanded on her conclusions a little. She could have linked the method's initial approach to learning music—by ear rather than through reading—to the way children learn language, which is a centerpiece of the Suzuki philosophy. She could have pointed out that teaching life skills (which she has discussed and applauded) and developing good citizens were greater priorities for Dr. Suzuki than training professional musicians. Unquestionably, she began too many sentences with "I," and phrases such as "some people say" (in the second sentence) are a bit too informal. But few essays, even published essays, are considered unimprovable by their authors, and in its current form this one illustrates much about persuasive writing and organization.

The idea that improvement is always possible, and always to be striven after, underlies a central point regarding revision: two drafts, a first and a final, even if the professor has annotated the first draft with suggestions for improvement, are not enough. Awkward passages and illogical changes of direction can be confusing to readers yet almost invisible to authors because the logic is, after all, their own—and they often need more than two drafts to find a problem. It is therefore advisable to outline the essay draft you consider to be final *after* it is written. This outline will demonstrate where transitions need to be used to guide the reader through the author's reasoning: *moreover, in contrast to, nonetheless, therefore,* and so on. In such an outline the building blocks of the essay will be apparent, and the author will then be able to use transitions to fashion a smooth and lucid paper, a real final draft.

Let us now turn to a somewhat longer and much more challenging essay, "Skryabin's Mystical Beliefs and the Holographic Model," by Jeff Simpson, an undergraduate piano major at the time this was written. A good deal of research went into this piece, as is apparent from both the material itself and the citations, but it is ultimately more essay than research paper because the author's primary purpose is to convince the reader of a particular point of view, which is that this composer and his music should be reexamined in the context of an entirely different branch of thought. A warning: close attention to basic content is necessary here, since quantum theory is not intuitive to most musicians.

Skryabin's Mystical Beliefs and the Holographic Model

by Jeff Simpson

Attitudes toward the musical contributions of the Russian composer and pianist Alexander Skryabin (1872–1915) have undergone stark transformations. The shift from resentment to awe is clearly evident in Dmitri Shostakovich when his 1931 assessment, "we consider Scriabin as our bitter musical enemy," later becomes "we are grateful to Scriabin for having expanded the boundaries of our art by his inexhaustible fantasy and his brilliant talent."[5] Skryabin's mystical beliefs have not enjoyed the same reconsideration. These beliefs are frequently tolerated as individual eccentricities rather than treated as a vivid, experiential understanding of reality. When we view Skryabin's mysticism in light of a much more recent and radically different model, however—the holographic theory of the physicist David Bohm—it becomes evident that Skryabin was accessing a more primary level of existence. We owe new consideration to this mysticism as a valuable perspective on the construction of reality.

[5][Simpson's note referenced a now-defunct link that was accessed February 13, 2000. As of December 2005, the same page can be found at *http://members. bellatlantic.net/~retemey/Scriabin/ScriabinCritics.html*. Fortunately, this quotation is known in the Skryabin literature, but this serves to illustrate a key complication with using Web sources: they move and disappear. This subject is addressed in greater detail in Chapter 6.]

Skryabin believed that the physical world was illusory and that a "more real" level existed. This deeper order was a total unity of collective consciousness. One of his journals states, "Individual consciousness differ only in their contents, but the bearers of these contents are identical. They are beyond space and time. We are faced here not with a multiplicity of conscious states, but with a universal consciousness that experiences a multitude of states of consciousness vertically (in time) and horizontally (in space)."[6] The universal consciousness was not just one of Skryabin's beliefs; he had direct access to this awareness as his mode of existence. His close friend Boris de Schloezer witnessed these transcendental states and described them, saying, "I watched him in such states of creative ecstasy. . . . All categories seemed to merge in him, and the structure of his personality seemed to vanish."[7] David Bohm shares this belief in a deeper order and offers some striking parallels to Skryabin.

Bohm's theory holds that the "reality of our everyday lives is really a kind of illusion, like a holographic image. Underlying it is a deeper order of existence, a vast and more primary level of reality that gives birth to all the objects and appearances of our physical world."[8] However, Bohm's model is not the result of mysticism; it is a product of quantum and theoretical physics.

Certain paradoxes in modern physics have prevented scientists from creating a comprehensive model of the universe. Bohm believed these illogical truths only existed when the conflicted objects were treated as separate entities acting autonomously. He

---

[6][Simpson's note] Boris de Schloezer, *Scriabin: Artist and Mystic,* trans. Nicolas Slonimsky (Berkeley and Los Angeles: University of California Press, 1987), 124.
[7][Simpson's note] Ibid., 101–02.
[8][Simpson's note] Michael Talbot, *The Holographic Universe* (New York: Harper-Perennial, 1992), 46.

argued that subatomic particles operate in a quantum field that is "non-local,"[9] meaning that distance does not exist. Without distance, the concept of separate identity is obliterated; thus, everything that exists must contain everything else. For Bohm, the paradox was resolved by interpreting the phenomena as separate expressions of a unified whole. Non-local reality was the implicate order. The universe of phenomena and individuality was an explicate order unfolding out of the implicate totality. The stumbling block for Bohm was deriving a structural model accounting for the abolition of distance. He found his solution in the holograph.

Holographic film contains wave interference patterns created by lasers.[10] Talbot summarizes the process this way: "A single laser light is split in two separate beams. The first beam is bounced off the object to be photographed. Then the second beam is allowed to collide with the reflected light of the first."[11] The image recorded resembles ripples in a pond and bears no resemblance to the subject being photographed. However, if a laser is focused on the film at the same angle as the laser used to create the pattern, the object photographed projects into three-dimensional space. Even more puzzling is the fact that a single piece of holographic film can theoretically hold an infinite number of images. By changing the angle of the laser hitting the film, separate images can be recorded and manifest in a cinematic succession. The fact that the complete wave interference pattern is uniformly

[9][Simpson's note] Ibid., 41.
[10][Simpson's note] The collision of any two wave-energies produces an interference pattern. Sonic pulses resulting from poor intonation—also known as "beats"—occur as out-of-phase waves periodically cancel and reinforce each other. As of 1992, a patent was pending for a method of holographically recording sound; Talbot discusses the inventor and provides further information. Talbot, 292–93.
[11][Simpson's note] Talbot, 14.

distributed in every part of the film is significant. If the film is cut into smaller pieces, any one piece will reproduce the entire image. Thus, the film is a static, non-local, *implicate* order where everything is contained in everything else. The projected hologram is the *explicate* order. If Bohm's model is correct, this movie is what we experience as our reality and daily lives.

Skryabin seems to have experienced this holographic process while composing the fifth sonata. "During the process of its composition," Schloezer recalled, "he felt as though he were projecting a three-dimensional body on a flat surface, stretching and flattening in time and space a prophetic vision that he experienced as an instant revelation, simplifying and at the same time impoverishing it."[12] The language and imagery used to describe this compositional process could easily be substituted with the description for taking a holographic photograph. Yet, it is important to note that the technology and scientific theory needed to create holograms did not exist until several decades after Skryabin's death. Schloezer's book was written between 1919 and 1921, leaving him with the same theoretical and technological void as Skryabin regarding this process. The significance of the vision as an instant revelation thus ties into non-locality: time is a function of distance divided by rate. If distance ceases to exist, time has no meaning. While in a transcendental state, Skryabin was able to instantly comprehend the sonata in its entirety because no other chronometry exists at that level. Support for this understanding of time as a static phenomenon is widely acknowledged among physicists and is embodied in the concept of "block-time."

A driving concept behind Skryabin's *Preparatory Act*—a work he intended as a mystical transformation of humanity—was fluidity

---

[12][Simpson's note] Schloezer, 86.

and the abandonment of concrete matter. Skryabin envisioned the set's architecture as a flowing design with shifting pieces and pillars of illuminated smoke. Tonally, the death harmonies—variants of the mystic chord—represent the flux between implicate and explicate orders. One music scholar states, "The *Preparatory Act* sketches contain sonorities that expand the qualities of musical stasis found in the mystic chord. They also symbolize in sound the implosion of time and space."[13] The mystic chord itself is a hybrid point of transition between a whole-tone scale, and octatonic scale, and a French sixth chord. It suspends our sense of place and becomes an allegory for non-local reality. Each of the three potential tonal destinations for the mystic chord becomes an unfolded hologram which can instantly flow into any of the other tonal realities by passing through the enfolded order of the chord.

Skryabin's music takes us to a distant landscape. Scholars, performers, and audiences have invested time and energy to appreciate his contribution to the arts, but it is appropriate now to put down the map and look at the scenery. Skryabin's music is the evocation, the theurgic ritual that transports us to his world of higher consciousness and unity, but it is his mystic understanding of reality that should be our primary concern. Schloezer states, "He was not creating this music out of nothing, . . . but rather he had removed a veil that obscured it, and thus made it visible."[14] To better understand the true message and quiddity of his art, the existence of a deeper order contained in Skryabin's mysticism deserves serious study and attention.

Before we even consider the argument, the composer's name requires explanation. The differences in orthography result from different

---

[13][Simpson's note] Simon Morrison, "Skryabin and the Impossible," *Journal of the American Musicological Society* 51/2 (1998), 315.
[14][Simpson's note] Schloezer, 85.

systems of transliterating the Russian (Cyrillic) alphabet. What was for a long time "Alexander Scriabin" is now, as found in the second edition of the *New Grove Dictionary of Music and Musicians* (2001), "Aleksandr Skryabin," and Simpson follows the latest practice but also leaves intact the spelling found in his sources. There are other ways of approaching disparities in spelling, such as tacitly changing older spellings or putting [sic] after each different use, but I agree with the author that in an essay, such apparatus seems needlessly clumsy, obsessive, and above all wasteful of precious space. (There was a length limit for this assignment.)

The issue of length has direct bearing on other authorial choices. Given the amount of historical and technical information that must be presented before an opinion could credibly be advanced, it is perhaps unavoidable that the essay has a certain density, and that some information that might be useful is not explained. One such example is the nature of Skryabin's mystic chord (a combination of two trichords, C–F♯–B♭ and E–A–D) and how it can function as a node between the whole-tone scale, the octatonic scale, and the French sixth chord. A more fundamental issue is that of metaphor: did Skryabin really *experience* the holographic process while composing the Fifth Sonata, or is the holographic process, rather, an apt metaphor for the sensation he did experience? He was creating an artwork, after all, in this world; it would take a good deal more to demonstrate that he actually experienced nonlocality and a kind of intersection between the posited deeper, primary reality and this world, which according to the theory is a world of appearances. Again, to incorporate an explanation of such a distinction would have proven very difficult logistically.

The real point of this kind of essay—and such views are not uncommon in the musical disciplines—is that there is a much better way (perhaps a radically different way) to view a subject or area that many consider to be well understood. In a difficult case such as this, the essential logic does not lie primarily in building a case to the author's conclusion ("we should all be looking at things *this* way!"), which is rather obvious, but rather in coherently linking the disparate but relevant parts of the author's view of the area itself. For this task, a different kind of outline is needed: one that connects to itself in a ringlike way. Excluding the introduction and conclusions, which may be summarized as "we don't know as much about X as we think" and "doesn't this make a lot more sense?", we might imagine this kind of rough outline for the essay:

1. Skryabin's mysticism: the belief in a deeper order of existence and shared consciousness

2. Striking similarity of Bohm's view: deeper reality as implicate order, and perceived reality as explicate (Plato here?
   In #1, better?)—quantum theory and nonlocality; holographic model

3. Modern holographic theory: definition, explanation

4. Similarity to Skryabin's experience composing; relationship
   to his mysticism as described in #1, and sonata-in-a-flash
   vision (like Mozart's)

5. Connection to broader view of Skryabin

The outline would then be refined, as was suggested with the previous essay. With regard to my fanciful parenthesis in (2), it would be natural for a student who had taken a Western civilization course to have encountered Plato's Theory of Forms, which holds that the Realm of Being
(where the Forms reside) is far more "real" than the Realm of Appearances (where *we* reside), where everything is a mere approximation of its
Form or Ideal. Similarly, the mention of Mozart in (4) touches base with
one of the most common myths of music history: that Mozart conceived
pieces in an instant and then had to spend time writing them down. I include these two ideas in this mock outline because they would be natural
ideas to occur to a student writing an essay on a musical subject, and because each would have been more trouble than it was worth to work into
the essay proper. To mention the Plato comparison would require the author to stress its relationship to that philosopher's moral philosophy, and
the Mozart myth seems to date from well after Skryabin's lifetime and
has only the most general relevance. Each would have taken space, in
other words—space the author didn't have to devote to it. Again, not
every initial idea or numbered item in an outline needs to make it to the
final draft. What this list does show is the interconnectedness of the
ideas: Skryabin's music and his mystical metaphysics; his metaphysics and
Bohm's theory of a deep, nonlocal reality; the relationship of that theory
to the holographic model (which is then explained); and finally the striking correspondence between these views of deeper reality and Skryabin's
experience composing, and what he was trying to express. From here
it's but a short step to "shouldn't we all be thinking about this?", with
the implied greater issue of "wouldn't *all* composers' beliefs and philosophies be relevant to how we study their music, rather than our more

comfortable approach of systematizing the notes they put on paper?" Such topics are uncomfortably broad, but are among the most pressing for writers on music to seek to address.

HINTS ON BEGINNING

The examination of finished essays and outlines like those that may have contributed to them leaves one crucial point unaddressed. Almost all writers, student and professional, feel that beginning is especially difficult. One philosophy even holds that one should begin by setting *anything* down on paper or computer screen, reasoning that it can always be changed, and that for this very reason one should not be too critical about the opening of a first draft. This approach aside, a well-chosen strategy or two for focusing an initial statement will help ensure that you make a strong beginning and move in the right direction. Acknowledging that even the most experienced authors sometimes find themselves stymied by an inability to begin (despite having much to say), here are some strategies to use when the pump, so to speak, needs to be primed.

Ask yourself questions. What is my main point? How do I set it up, or engage the reader in thinking about it? Do I lay out the data or arguments leading to it right away, or after an introduction? These questions are analogous to those a writer of a different sort of paper might ask: how does the musical work I am discussing compare to other works of the same genre/from the same era/on the same concert? When a live performance is being discussed, how am I different from the way I was when I entered the hall? Why, in short, am I writing this? ("Because the silly thing is assigned," true or not, will not get you out of the starting blocks.)

If the opening is proving to be a major hurdle, don't begin with the first sentence or paragraph. Even with best-laid plans, the first few versions of an opening paragraph are often discarded. Why, if stalled at the beginning, allow a difficulty with the opening to prevent you from making any progress whatsoever? Start with the second paragraph, or the second sentence, or anything you feel confident writing about *right now*. Perhaps this is background, or analysis, or even conclusions; regardless, begin writing at any point in the outline. The holes can be filled in later.

In the initial stages, do not be too self-critical. It is best for an author to complete a draft, one that covers the basic content from first to last, and then to start the revising process. Being compulsive about revising and correcting an opening paragraph or section as soon as it is written is less advisable; the subsequent lack of attention to other parts of the paper will show in the final product. Keep writing until you have a whole to work with, even if it is initially somewhat sloppy and misshapen.

Remember: the final draft of an essay (indeed, of any piece of writing) is a kind of performance. This is the version of your work presented for evaluation to the public—or to at least one reader—and this is the version that will leave a final impression. How many of us have thought ruefully, after a performance, "But it went *fine* in the practice room!"? In writing we are more fortunate; the "performance" does not happen in real time. The editing process is comparable, rather, to preparing a digital recording: the wrong notes can be removed, the phrasing can be recalibrated, the awkward moments softened into the desired result. In the editing process the "performer" can say "sorry; let me do that a bit better" with impunity as many times as necessary. For performing musicians, that is an unimagined luxury.

But authors pay for this privilege with patience and time. Because most of the writing process consists of revision—writing being, in large part, a matter of rewriting—it is a multistep process that cannot profitably be hurried. Fine writing requires good organization and a strong rough draft as building blocks, certainly, but most of all it requires persistent, patient editing, with much reading aloud and self-evaluation. In other words, you will produce many drafts, and your vigilance in critiquing them cannot flag. As this phase requires time and patience above all, it is necessary to get to it as soon as possible.

6

RESEARCH IN MUSIC

It is the rare music student indeed who rejoices at the announcement of a written assignment or term paper.[1]

—JOHN E. DRUESEDOW, JR.

Although research papers, program notes, reviews, and critical essays all have different primary goals, they also have a good deal in common; each of these genres utilizes both research and critical evaluation. The distinctions are of emphasis rather than of kind: an essay is primarily a persuasive exercise, but it needs to be based on facts; program notes are primarily a presentation of general background research targeted at the music lover rather than a more specialized reader; and the research paper is primarily a presentation of specific, academic research in coherent, digested form.

This chapter addresses the research process in music, from the choice of topic to the gathering of material to organization to written presentation.

THE PURPOSES OF RESEARCH

Students too often look upon the musical scholarship they read in books and journals as something to be neither questioned nor used as a model, seeing it instead as the intimidating product of higher, perhaps more boring but certainly wholly alien, intellects. Music researchers, therefore,

---

[1]John E. Druesedow, Jr., *Library Research Guide to Music* (Ann Arbor, MI: Pierian Press, 1982), 1.

are perceived to be fundamentally separate from other musicians and the musical world. Researching, a skill that will prove invaluable in a musical lifetime, is feared and avoided. This is wrong, but widespread.

Far better is the idea of a continuum. There is no essential difference between student research and professional research, for they share the goal of enhancing the understanding of both researcher and readers. In a college course, this means the understanding of the student author-researcher, perhaps the class, and even the professor. (The professor may well learn something about the subject and will certainly learn about the student author's understanding of it.) When writing for publication, the goal is to enlighten a certain kind of reader: an article in a magazine will seek to enlighten one group of readers, and an article in a scholarly journal or book will aim at another group. But with all topics, from the most widely studied to the most obscure, each author offers something unique, and so may be said to make a contribution to the field, even when the contribution is simply a clear summary and presentation of others' published research. For the undergraduate, seeing yourself as a member of the broad authorial and research family enables you to identify more and more with the wider musical world and to find a place within it without limiting your view to the immediate environment of practice-room, class-room, or department.

CHOICE OF TOPIC

In many courses you will be assigned a topic or told to choose your own topic within assigned parameters. When you have no immediate affinity for your topic, don't waste time feeling resentful. Think of your task the way you would think of practicing études, or learning or teaching repertoire that does (yet) not have your full sympathy. In performance, every work is your favorite work in the world, and every style has your most profound commitment. So it is with writing; regardless of the topic or the extent of your commitment, every stage of the process requires your absolute best.

If you do have leeway in choosing a topic, write about the subject matter closest to your heart. Such a choice may involve a particular work or kind of music, a musical issue or question, or any of a number of related areas, but it is best to proceed from your own passion. The worst course of action is to choose a topic on the basis of what you think the professor would like to see, or the supposed ease of completion, or the simplicity of the issue involved. The goal of "just getting it done" is no more acceptable than the goal of a barely acceptable performance of a Mozart piano concerto would be.

A common mistake is the choice of a topic that is too broad. Topics such as "American Indian Music," "Nicolò Paganini: Life and Music," and "The Blues Roots of Rock and Roll" may initially seem promising, but a tremendous amount of research has already been done in those areas, and a college- or even graduate-level research paper on such a broad topic could only be a collection of somewhat random facts that do not lead in a particular direction. A wiser approach would be to narrow the field, resulting in a topic such as "Cherokee Courtship Songs," "Paganini the Composer," or "Robert Johnson's Influence on English Blues-Rock." Answering a specific how or why question or addressing some other specific task can focus research more easily than trying to produce an "overview" paper. Setting boundaries can help ensure that the researcher does not become rudderless after the research process is already well underway.

If, conversely, a topic is too narrow, you can broaden the scope by expanding the time period in question, looking at related repertoire or additional composers, or asking different questions about the context in which the music under discussion appeared. Ultimately, whether a topic is too narrow or too broad depends in large part on the author's background and the length of the assignment. Self-awareness and forethought are therefore indispensable tools in the early stages of research.

LOCATING SOURCES

Most people now have access to online library catalogues—searchable electronic databases. Predictably, the protocols for using these tools differ widely, including their uses of keywords, their ability to accommodate Boolean searches (i.e., those in which the desired words or character strings relate to each other in ways described by *and*, *or*, and *not*), and any number of other variables. Each system and search protocol must be mastered, and this is a matter of time and experience. For example, searching *strauss orchestration* in some systems might identify sources with those words in the title, or (better) subject headings, but in others would only show sources with that exact string of characters, which are likely to be few. Trying a variety of different search strategies is always necessary, and the more creative you are, the more sources you will find. (More on resourcefulness in the search process below.) Suffice to say, if you are not finding any information at all on your topic, the problem is likely to be with your search strategy, not a complete absence of information on a topic in your library or the available electronic databases.

KINDS OF WRITTEN SOURCES

Publications about music (that is, books and articles), musical scores themselves, and sound recordings are all sources—sources to be used very differently—and these sources (and a great deal else) may be available in electronic form. Here are four truths regarding sources:

- There is a huge amount of source material available.
- The number of sources is constantly growing.
- No source is 100% dependable.
- No single source is completely duplicated by another.

It is safe neither to trust any single source implicitly nor to ignore any sources you have at your disposal. As many sources as possible must be critically examined. The task of the researcher is not only to be aware of and familiar with the relevant sources, but to be able to evaluate each and use it accordingly. (The idea of evaluation is discussed below.)

Non-English Sources

In music, research material directly relevant to your work is not always published in English. For this reason, the ability to access literature in foreign languages is a great advantage. The available English-language sources will usually be sufficient for undergraduate research topics, although if you are studying a foreign language it would be a great idea to try your linguistic wings on a source or two in that language. For graduate-level research, or research intended for publication, access to foreign-language sources is a necessity, either through using your own skills (which always benefit from practice) or, less ideally, with the help of a friend or professional translator. Much depends on the topic: for example, virtually all the important sources on the Spanish composer Joaquín Rodrigo are in Spanish, so it is hard to imagine any research on him by someone with no capability in that language. By contrast, a good deal of the most important research on composers such as Bach and Mozart is written in English, so one could certainly say that it is as important for a German or Austrian researcher studying those composers to know English as it is for English and

North American researchers to know German. The truth is that language skills are necessary for any ongoing work in music research. That said, we will proceed to a short survey of English-language sources.

Reference Sources

The first stop for any research project needs to be one (or more) of the major reference works in music. Among the benefits of this is the clarification of concepts central to your project but perhaps not all that common outside it (that is, the huge gray area between "common knowledge" and the specifics you will be researching and citing); you want to have a good sense for this *before* the project is well under way. The information in standard reference works is the product, for the most part, of relatively recent scholarship (although, of course, our understanding deepens all the time, and no source is error-free). Bibliographies of relevant books and articles are often provided, offering a variety of fruitful places to look next.

The standard English-language music reference work is *The New Grove Dictionary of Music and Musicians*, second edition, edited by Stanley Sadie, in 29 volumes (London: Macmillan, 2001). More an encyclopedia than a dictionary, this compendious work is built upon the first edition (1980), but that earlier edition was descended more distantly from the several different editions of *Grove's Dictionary of Music and Musicians*, the first of which appeared in 1879. The 1980 edition of the *New Grove* had several spin-off series: the *New Grove Dictionary of Musical Instruments* (1984), the *New Grove Dictionary of American Music* (1986), the *New Grove Dictionary of Jazz* (1988), and the *New Grove Dictionary of Opera* (1992). The *New Grove* is now also available online, on a subscription basis, in a continually updated format. Rock and pop music has a similar work: the *Encyclopedia of Popular Music*, second edition, compiled and edited by Colin Larkin, in eight volumes (New York: Muze UK, 1998). The equivalent work for world music is *The Garland Encyclopedia of World Music* (New York: Garland, 1998). Musical terminology may be found in the *New Harvard Dictionary of Music*, third edition, edited by Don Randel (Cambridge, MA: Harvard University Press, 1986), and musicians and musical figures can be found in *Baker's Biographical Dictionary of Musicians*, eighth edition, edited by Nicolas Slonimsky (New York: Schirmer, 1992).

The preceding is only the shortest of short lists; further help on navigating the thousands of reference works available in music may be found by consulting Phillip D. Crabtree and Donald H. Foster, *Sourcebook for Research in Music* (Bloomington, IN: Indiana University Press, 1993),

Vincent H. Duckles and Ida Reed, *Music Reference and Research Materials: An Annotated Bibliography*, fifth edition (New York: Schirmer, 1997), or a good reference librarian. Even better, browse the reference shelf before consulting the librarian; first learn as much as you can on your own. Before approaching a librarian, make sure you have already made an intelligent, good-faith effort to find at least the basic information yourself.

Books

Articles in reference works often include bibliographies, and this is true with many of the articles in the *New Grove II* (as it is informally known; this is not appropriate for formal citations unless you are specifically told it will suffice for an abbreviated format). The moment a bibliography is printed, however, it is closed to new and potentially important entries. Older sources are by no means automatically superseded by later ones, but it is not safe to rely on them when further research has been carried out. In general, one should start with the most recent work, from which a sense of the entire body of research ought to emerge. (The section Relative Age of Sources below will offer more thoughts on this issue.)

Before taking the next step, you need to have a solid familiarity with the music to be studied. It is expected, then, that you will already have the scores and have listened to recordings—ideally, several different recordings, so that you can compare them. Do not underestimate the importance of this step; your written sources may well assume that the reader is already familiar with the music, so using them before you have achieved this familiarity will only mean you have to return and read them again.

After you have perused the reference works and are familiar with the music, your next visit to the music library is likely to net you several books relevant to your topic. Let us say that you are studying Liszt's Sonata in B Minor for piano. You locate the Liszt section and immediately find at least one book entirely devoted to the piece, plus a number of other substantial-looking books, several of which (you learn from the tables of contents and indexes) have lengthy passages, or even entire chapters, about the piece. Given this bounty, you may be tempted to believe that you are done collecting material. But wait: completely different perspectives may await you in books on the piano sonata (in general), on Hungarian music (Liszt is still probably Hungary's most famous composer), and on nineteenth-century "Music of the Future" (Liszt and Wagner being the most prominent exponents of this school), to name only three areas.

So, in seeking out relevant books, it is necessary to approach a research topic from several different directions. Often the most helpful information will be gleaned from books that initially seem to be only tangentially related to your topic.

Do not forget collections of correspondence, autobiographical material, and primary-source documentation. Although an individual's first-person testimony may not be any more trustworthy than other sources (memories may fade, translations may mislead, and a particular version of a story may seem more attractive to the author than what actually happened), it offers yet another angle of approach to a musical work, person, or question. When a particular work is being studied, *always* look for it in the index to the composer's published correspondence, and even if it does not appear, read as much as possible about that portion of the composer's life.

Journal and Magazine Articles

Much of the periodical literature is *juried* or *peer-reviewed*, equivalent terms meaning that before an article is published, it is read and approved by the editor of the publication and one or more outside readers in order to make sure that it meets the scholarly and literary standards of the publication. This process of course cannot guarantee the veracity of every word published—which remains the author's responsibility—but the additional scholarly oversight does offer further assurance of quality. It is harder to establish quality with nonjuried publications, such as many newsletters; since there is no guarantee of external reading or approval their veracity might depend entirely on the scholarly method and integrity of each individual author, or there may still be substantial editorial oversight. Scholarly newsletters (such as the *Newsletter of the American Brahms Society*) tend to be as dependable as juried publications simply because they function as scholarly journals; they are usually produced by scholars and have scholarly contributions, but they serve the needs of a narrower group of readers than a journal would.

For all but the most superficial research projects, the periodical literature must be scoured for relevant articles. The same observations about directly and indirectly related book sources apply here, too, so for information on Brahms, for example, you would have to look at more periodicals than the *Newsletter of the American Brahms Society*, helpful and relevant though it will be. Other angles, in addition to scholarly theory and history journals, might include publications on piano music (or chamber music, the symphony, choral music, etc.), nineteenth-century music, or theory and analysis. A sober reminder is in order here: music as a field does not enjoy some of the resources that other fields do. Although the entire historical periodical literature in some professions is almost completely indexed (and others have most of the publications themselves available online), there is currently no single database that encompasses the whole of the music periodical literature. Despite the fact that music as a discipline is considerably behind better-funded fields, though, the situation is improving, and both print and electronic databases are available.

For the last few decades, two print sources have been standard: *The Music Index: A Subject-Author Guide to Music Periodical Literature* (Detroit: Information Services, 1949–63; Detroit: Information Coordinators, 1963–87; Warren, MI: Harmonie Park Press [Information Coordinators], 1987–), and *RILM Abstracts of Music Literature/Répertoire internationale de la littérature musicale* (New York: International Musicological Society, the Association of Music Libraries, Archives, and Document Centers, and the International Council for Traditional Music, 1967–). *The Music Index* provides article citations for a wide variety of music periodicals, including review citations indexed by the subject of the review. *RILM Abstracts* provides citations and abstracts not only for periodical articles, but also for books on music, master's theses, and doctoral dissertations. Both of these databases are available online and are far easier to use electronically.

A more recent, online-only resource is the *International Index of Music Periodicals* (Chadwyck-Healey, Inc.), a highly useful searchable database, with brief abstracts as well as citations for articles on musical subjects (though it tends to be weighted toward recording and performance reviews). For locating relevant articles in the historical periodical literature, there are both print and online versions of *RIPM*, the Retrospective Index to Music Periodicals/*Répertoire international de la presse musicale*, which covers roughly 1800–1950. Of course, it is impossible for such a database to be exhaustive, given the sheer number of European periodicals, but it is still an invaluable resource for locating *contemporary* commentary about historical music, performers, and institutions.

Other Web-Based Sources

Databases aside, the World Wide Web is making an ever-increasing amount of material available in this, the so-called Information Age. As mentioned before, some of this material duplicates or updates (with much greater convenience) print resources such as the *New Grove Dictionary*, the *RILM* and *RIPM Abstracts*, and the *Music Index*. Because of the ephemerality of any electronic medium, I recommend consulting electronic resources in addition to those in print, *not* as an alternative. Unfortunately, sometimes severe financial constraints force libraries to opt for virtual resources rather than those in print. The basic principle is to look at anything and everything you can! To my knowledge, *no music periodical database is complete*, and so it follows that no database exhaustively duplicates another.

World Wide Web pages may be owned and administered by a company, an organization, a scholar, a hobbyist, any private individual: anyone with access to the required computer resources. A tremendous amount of information may be found on Web pages, the format of which lends itself to people with specific, somewhat narrow interests. One might learn more about the French Revolutionary composer François-Joseph Gossec, for example, from a Web site devoted to his life and music than from a general reference source that has to be judicious about the space it devotes to minor masters. There is no guarantee of oversight, though, and despite the amount of information readily available, variations in quality and dependability can be extreme.

Issues of accuracy and scholarly dependability are even more immediate with Wiki-based sources such as wikipedia.com. A Wiki is a piece of server or database software that allows any and all users to make changes in content. Wikipedia.com, perhaps the most well known of these sites, is like a huge encyclopedia with articles written by those with appropriate expertise, and indeed a tremendous amount of value is to be found there. This "democratization of the Web" is an idealistic—indeed, utopian—approach, but its price is that no editorial oversight is in place to prevent misinformation from being posted and disseminated. Such a thing might be the result of an author's practical joke, the desire to slander someone living or dead, or just a partisan insistence on some issue or other, but the Wiki structure means that any user has control over the content. It follows that any information gleaned from a Wiki-based site can range from authoritative to fraudulent. Anything found on such a site must therefore be corroborated elsewhere, and should not be used and cited independently of other sources. (More on source criticism below.)

Recording Liner Notes

Almost all sound recordings come with some kind of explanatory material, and there is nothing wrong (in principle) with utilizing it in the research process. That said, a warning of *caveat lector* ("Let the reader beware") is in order. Many recordings have excellent notes, but others do not; authors can be hobbled by the limited space provided, or told to write on a *very* general level, or (worst of all) told to lighten it up and be entertaining. Sometimes recording companies seem to feel that liner notes are not important enough to warrant a competent author in the first place. Notes often tend to be general, rightly targeted at the music-purchasing public rather than a research audience, so they cannot serve as the backbone source of a project. Still, helpful information is often to be found in these sources, and first-rank scholars are sometimes engaged to write them. There are no guarantees either way, so the only safe comment to make is that with practice, you will develop good instincts about the quality of what you read.

Musical Scores

Almost any research on a musical topic requires the examination of musical scores. All scores are not, however, created equal; different kinds of scores are produced with different purposes in mind. More discussion of this point follows in Use of Sources, below; for now it will suffice to describe several varieties of scores.

An *Urtext* is an edition that seeks to transmit, as faithfully and exactly as possible, what the composer put on the manuscript page and/or what appeared in the earliest editions, those presumably under the composer's control, without editorial intrusions of any kind. Frequently the explanatory notes of the Urtext editions address variant readings and differences between sources. A *performance edition* provides not only the composer's score but also an editor's recommendations for performance. These may include (in addition to whatever indications the composer provided) suggestions on phrasing, fingering, bowing, articulation, ornamentation, and general performance instructions and metronome marks. (A hybrid is the *critical edition*, or *scholarly performance edition*, which seeks to marry scholarly accuracy of the score with informed recommendations regarding historical performance practices.) *Study scores* are generally low-budget reprints of earlier editions (miniature scores fall into this category); their goal is to make available a maximum amount of music for the minimum cost. They are intended neither as performing editions nor as last-word scholarly documents. *Collected works* editions, found primarily in libraries, seek to include a composer's entire output in a single, multivolume edition. Related to collected works are *monumental editions*, also intended primarily for libraries, which include generally hard-to-find works by a variety of historical composers (especially so-called *Kleinmeister*, minor masters). Famous examples of monumental sets include *Denkmäler der Tonkunst in Osterreich* (Monuments of Musical Art in Austria) and *Musica Britannica*. Scholarly accuracy is a central goal of both collected works and monumental editions, but since scholars continue working in these areas, the accuracy of this work tends to come under debate relatively quickly.

For learning the contents of collected works and monumental editions, the best source is still Anna Harriet Heyer, *Historical Sets, Collected Editions, and Monuments of Music*, second edition (Chicago: American Library Association, 1980), in two volumes. A newer version, edited by George Hill and Norris Stephens, appeared in 1997; it incorporates the contents of sets published since 1980, but does not include the complete contents of the earlier edition. The two versions are organized in different ways, and require a certain amount of practice. When this information is all available electronically, as Hill and Stephens suggest it will be, that will potentially be the most efficient format.

USE OF SOURCES

Optimizing Research Time

Working intelligently is far better than working hard. As you go through your steadily increasing pile of sources, you may begin to suspect that it will be impossible to complete your project (or any project) before the due date, or for that matter before your graduation! Just to read six available biographies would take more time than you have. Isn't there, you wonder, a better way?

This is where a revelation occurs: you do not need to read, word for word, every source that looks like it may have something promising. Skimming sources for relevant material is one of the researcher's most essential skills. When you research a particular piece or pieces, start with a basic understanding of the composer's biography (such as may be found in *New Grove II*, or in a recently published biography) and then proceed to tables of contents and indexes, looking for information on your piece. Find the years in which the piece was composed and examine the passages dealing with that time period for relevant information. The same is true when you research a person or a problem rather than a particular piece; save time by using safe, dependable shortcuts.

Don't Believe Everything You Read!

Caveat lector again—this warning is as valuable today as it has ever been. Virtually every source, from the most scholarly to the most popularized, contains errors. Unfortunately, authors have different standards of accuracy, and although a book's main area of focus may be rigorously documented and presented, ancillary material may be somewhat more casually handled. You may doubt that a student or other pre-professional would be able to judge the merit of published works (or even have the gall to attempt it), but you are well within your rights and capabilities in learning to do so.

Imagine that you want to do a research paper on a favorite 1960s rock group, and you find the group discussed in great detail in a book that seeks to prove that rock is the greatest evil of the modern era: the pernicious product of hostile foreign influences, the devil, or both. (Such books do exist.) Would you trust the author's comments about your favorite group? Must you, because this book is in print, quote it and treat its content as fact, or at least as worth addressing? To choose a less extreme example, imagine that you are interested in, say, the masses of a certain Renaissance composer. You find contradictory information in two books, one a general history of Western music, the other a more specialized study of this composer's works. You must ask: when were the two sources written, and which is more likely to be right? You will have to check additional sources in hopes of identifying the error and avoiding it, whoever made it. And this leaves aside the different interpretive conclusions, presented with due authorial assurance, that will be drawn by different writers about the same musical works or music-related issues. Although there is no surefire method, particularly for students, for evaluating unfamiliar sources, the principles explained above will aid in this process and will enable your research instincts to become ever more dependable.

Scholarly vs. Textbook Sources

Sources need to be evaluated with their particular goals kept in mind. General sources and more specialized scholarly sources differ in a variety of ways, and they cannot be understood as equivalent. For example, one standard general history textbook states, "The vocal forms of the Renaissance were marked by smoothly gliding melodies conceived for the voice."[2] What does the student researcher then make of some of the early secular vocal works of the fifteenth-century composer Guillaume Du Fay, which can be highly syncopated, rhythmically complex, and difficult enough to require a virtuoso vocal technique? What of the sometimes frenetic and mercurial melodic lines of the late-Renaissance madrigals of Carlo Gesualdo? But these counterexamples do not negate the idea that, in general, a good part of the vocal aesthetic of Renaissance church music had to do with smoothness, seamlessness, and the creation of melodies that were not only gratifying to sing but resonated well within the acoustic spaces of churches and cathedrals, where voices were frequently heard.

Remember, general sources provide a *general* background; they prepare the reader for further work by presenting a broad overall context, but they cannot be read as if their information were as specifically true as that in specialized studies. This caveat applies also to articles in periodicals; the goals and approach of (for example) an article appearing in a magazine for voice teachers must be kept in mind when comparing its contents with those of an article in a research journal.

Relative Age of Sources

Although certain older sources such as Manfred Bukofzer's *Music in the Baroque Era* (quoted in Chapter 3) remain immensely valuable, relying on them may be risky because of the extent to which later research has transformed the field. Older sources may also reflect antiquated and parochial perspectives. But reliance on modern sources, too, carries risks. Modern sources may be shaped and informed by fashionable but ephemeral critical or aesthetic perspectives, and are further removed from historical subjects than older sources are. So, although we may be properly cautious of older sources' presumed narrowness and antiquation, modern sources can themselves be firmly and confidently based on cultural suppositions alien to the subject in question.

The positive side of this two-part warning is that both older and more modern sources have, at least potentially, specific strengths. Older sources are closer to the worldview and zeitgeist of the music of recent centuries, and they may have the benefit of more oral history (such as authors' interviews with people involved with or witness to the music,

---

[2]Joseph Machlis and Kristine Forney, *The Enjoyment of Music*, 7th ed., Chronological version (New York: W. W. Norton, 1995), 99.

person, or issue under discussion). Further, an older source may be the product of a mind so insightful that it remains valuable no matter what particulars are altered by subsequent research. (The writings of Paul Henry Lang, Donald Francis Tovey, and—again—Manfred Bukofzer come to mind.) Modern sources usually aspire to modern scholarly standards, seek to take all relevant source material and previous research into account, and aim to arrive at critical conclusions based on evidence, and this may well make them more dependable—for most users—and inclusive than earlier efforts.

How much of this is true for each source will vary. The only generalizations it is safe to make are that the age of a source informs what and how it is able to communicate, and that all sources must be used by researchers with a critical stance in mind.

Authorial Perspective

The evaluation of not only authors but also their agendas is a vital task for the researcher, who seeks above all not to be misled. A modern reader will be surprised to find conversations among long-dead historical figures and detailed descriptions of historical events in certain older sources—and even in some newer ones—and still may (mistakenly) consider such sources trustworthy. Some decades ago, fabricating conversations and other historical details in order to produce a "good read" was acceptable. I would say, rather, that the presence of such material is sufficient grounds to consider a source highly suspect. Similar are those cases where the authors of books and articles approach a subject from a specific polemical position, such as that the essence of Chopin's character may be seen in his religious beliefs,[3] or that rock music is habitually laced with subliminal messages that range from commercially manipulative to satanic,[4] or that Arnold Schoenberg's views of the "emancipation of dissonance" were based on poor history and a personal agenda.[5] Authors who approach their musical subjects from the perspective of proving such all-encompassing points are best viewed

---

[3]Mateusz Gliński, *Chopin the Unknown* (Windsor, ONT: Assumption University of Windsor Press, 1963).

[4]Dan and Steve Peters, with Cher Merrill, *Rock's Hidden Persuader: The Truth about Backmasking* (Minneapolis: Bethany House, 1985).

[5]William Thomson, *Schoenberg's Error* (Philadelphia: University of Pennsylvania Press, 1991).

from a distance. Their goals are narrow, and scholarly rigor is frequently of secondary importance.

Dependability of the Source Itself

The more research one does, the more one develops a sense about the dependability of sources. Many people love music, many people produce it in some way, and (more to the point) many write about it, regardless of training, knowledge, or any other standard prerequisite. Music is a subject about which people with no training or practical experience often feel they have a good deal to say simply because they listen to it a lot and it gives them pleasure. Books and articles by both the trained and the untrained may look credible on first examination, regardless of whether the writings have had appropriate evaluation, editorial guidance, or oversight before publication.

As discussed earlier, the World Wide Web is even more problematic, its potential benefits notwithstanding. The democratization of information—anyone can set up a Web site and say virtually anything—makes it incumbent on researchers to be as critical as possible of the information they find there. Many Web sites are owned and administered by private citizens, and any monitoring for quality or accuracy is up to them. There is nothing to prevent a junior high or high school student from deciding to put everything she or he knows about the blues on a Web site—nor should there be—but the danger lies in a reader's uncritical trust in the information found there. It is easy to assume that anyone who takes the trouble to write, either on paper or on the Web, knows something about the subject—particularly when slick, professional-looking graphics and interfaces are involved in the presentation—but nothing could be further from the truth. This is why "I picked this up off the Web" is one of the least convincing defenses for any otherwise undefended information. It is not that information on private Web sites is automatically wrong; it is that there is nothing to *prevent* it from being wrong, and that it is necessary to corroborate it with other sources. Again, although there are no guarantees, juried sources are likely to be more dependable than nonjuried ones.

Special Difficulties in Using Musical Sources

In using and evaluating any source, always keep the focus of the project itself in clear view. This focus, more than anything else, will facilitate the accurate assessment of the source's relevance or authority for the purposes at hand. Sources may be virtually unimpeachable as far as their intended uses, but through misuse or misinterpretation they may still lead the novice researcher astray. Among those most often misused are musical scores.

Let us say that a student-researcher wants to establish, as closely as possible, how J. S. Bach believed a particular sarabande for keyboard ought to be performed. Should this student go to the original manuscript or to an Urtext, a presumably faithful reproduction (in published form) of the score, exactly as the composer notated the work? The premise here would be that the score alone is as complete for today's reader as it was for Bach's contemporaries, that anything that Bach did not explicitly notate, a modern performer need not know. Is this a safe assumption for music written between 250 and 300 years ago? We know that musicians of Bach's time would have known and practiced certain performance conventions, from specific and idiomatic rhythmic realizations (such as *notes inégales*) to ways of ornamenting (for example, on repeats) and of achieving dynamic variation using the different manuals of a harpsichord. Neither the composer's manuscript nor a published Urtext would provide any of this information, and a student-researcher would be dangerously underinformed.

Is our student better off, then, with an edited musical score? Perhaps; perhaps not. Editors can provide explanatory notes and informed suggestions for phrasings, fingerings, ornamentation, and other matters, but they can also mislead by such prescriptions. A keyboard fingering conceived by a pianist today for digital ease and dependability might completely confound another player's hand, the phrasing of the period, and in any case be unworkable on a harpsichord, clavichord, or organ (the keyboard instruments of Bach's time). Suggested ornamentation in Baroque or Classic music, about which there is always much debate, might be far too conservative or too florid. What is more, our understanding of Baroque phrasing, fingering, and other performance considerations has changed a great deal since many highly edited nineteenth-century performance editions were produced, and it continues to change. The most recent available edition, then? Maybe, but who is to say that that one editor had all the answers? One recent edition of J. S. Bach's *Well-Tempered Clavier* so carefully and thoroughly provided all kinds of information that it became easy to ignore editorial markings because there were so many of them—a complete defeat of the purpose.[6] Moral: *nothing* is completely safe, or

[6]J. S. Bach, *The Well-Tempered Clavier*, vol. I, ed. Willard Palmer (Sherman Oaks, CA: Alfred Publishing, 1981).

completely dependable, or useful in every situation. The researcher arrives at the information needed by constantly interrogating the sources, asking of each source only the questions appropriate to it, finding other sources for the unanswered questions, collecting and collating information, and drawing interpretive conclusions based on the critical appraisal of all available information.

Recordings, too, offer less "proof" than they sometimes seem to. It is tempting, particularly for students, to feel that a particular point about a work is "proven"—how much ornamentation to use, what tempo is appropriate, or just "how it sounds"—by a persuasive recording, particularly if it is by a famous artist or ensemble. But an individual recording actually proves very little about a work. In one way, it is like a live performance: x amount of ornamentation may be appropriate, but the recording "proves" only that it worked *in this one performance*. Traditional, non-historically-informed readings of Baroque works may seem persuasive, and indeed the performers' artistry may make them so, but this does not "prove" anything about how the music was or is to be performed.

That music has been interpreted and recorded a certain way is no assurance that this is the way the music was conceived. For example, Jelly Roll Morton's recordings of Scott Joplin's *Maple Leaf Rag* are fascinating historical documents (and great pieces of playing to boot), but they tell us far more about the pianist and his background and taste than about Joplin and the classic piano rag. The same can be said of Vladimir Horowitz's recordings of Scarlatti, and of any number of other recorded performances. Recordings, even those *by* a composer or made under the composer's control, have few prescriptive applications. The critical acumen of the listener, and the ability to read a score and understand musical context, are of primary importance in using recordings.

There are, then, far more questions to be asked than there are answers to be depended upon. This is a good thing! Although it may initially make the research process seem intimidating, even impossible, what it really indicates is that research is a living, vibrant activity. Important materials are always being discovered, and important issues are always benefiting from reframed questions, more insightful consideration, and new perspectives. Not only do we learn more daily, we consider and reflect with more skill and wisdom daily. There are no questions that are so settled they do not need to be revisited, and no closed books in music research.

CITING YOUR SOURCES

Few research issues are as important as the proper use and citation of your sources. Citations enable you to tell the reader which of the ideas in your work originated with someone else, and where they might be found. (Citation forms are found in Chapter 9.) It is no crime to base your work on that of others; virtually every piece of research is founded, one way or another, on research that came before. But the failure to cite sources, which amounts to taking credit for another's thoughts—whether intentionally or inadvertently, whether the material is directly quoted or paraphrased—is *plagiarism*. Plagiarism is a crime in the publishing world and an actionable offense in colleges and universities, where standard penalties range from an automatic failing grade in the course to more lasting disciplinary action, including expulsion. Dishonesty is unforgivable; unfortunately, in matters of citation, carelessness is often indistinguishable from dishonesty. There is no margin for error in issues of academic integrity.

But does an author need to footnote every thought not explicitly his or her own? Of course not. All direct quotes require citation, as do specific facts that lie outside so-called common knowledge, such as: "In the Yardbirds 'Heart Full of Soul,' Jeff Beck based his guitar hook on the playing of a sitarist who was on an earlier take." Whether the writer has heard one of the outtakes from the recording session or read this fact somewhere, it needs to be cited. But matters of common knowledge should not be cited, even when they are new to novice researchers. This is a gray area, and not all authorities or writing instructors agree on what constitutes common knowledge, or on how rigorous student-authors need to be. (In academic circumstances, the instructor's preferences prevail in this matter.) Consider this sentence:

> George Gershwin was born in New York City in 1898 to immigrant parents, and began his musical career at a New York publishing house, playing through songs for prospective interpreters.

The information contained in such a sentence need not be cited, because it is available in countless biographical treatments of the composer and is neither new nor debatable. If you were to quote the sentence directly, you would certainly have to cite the source because the words would not be your own, but there is no reason that this sort of sentence should be quoted rather than paraphrased.

To Quote or to Paraphrase?

You will most often be quoting primary sources, such as historical documents or the comments or reminiscences of historical figures. Such direct quotations are splendid for making or supporting a point, but you should never assume that they need no explanation. What seems to you like an obvious connection may strike the reader as a non sequitur, so you must always provide commentary: before the quotation, some kind of lead-in that prepares the reader for what the quotation will explain or illustrate, and after it a transition to your next point. Paraphrasing is best for secondary sources (such as articles or books by scholars); such sources should only be quoted when you want to discuss or take specific issue with an author's formulation or view of the subject, such as when you need to address George Bernard Shaw's view of Brahms's *German Requiem* rather than the piece itself. Matters of fact, such as the sentence about Gershwin above, should be paraphrased, whether common knowledge or not. Finally, when another's words perfectly encapsulate the point you wish to make—be the original from the Bible, from Shakespeare, or from another writer about music—the passage can and should be quoted and cited. This kind of quotation often seems to culminate a discussion, and the change of authorial voice is an effective literary technique, when judiciously used.

TURNING RESEARCH INTO WRITING

The Foundations of Your Research

The research process is in one sense never-ending, but it does need to come to some kind of conclusion so that you can begin to write your paper. At the point you begin to write, you should feel ready to do so: both formative and specific research are completed, and you are prepared not only to view your subject in a proper context but also to arrive at some conclusions as a result of evaluating the evidence. Inevitably, minor issues will still crop up, and you will have to look things up throughout the writing process. But waiting until the research process is as complete as possible before you begin to write will help ensure that your overview of the subject will not undergo radical changes.

That confidently said, it is common for an important source or a major piece of information to pop up unexpectedly during the writing process—perhaps a late arrival from Interlibrary Loan, perhaps a professor's offhand comment that points to a new direction, perhaps a realization of your own. Major revising and recasting, unforeseen and unscheduled, may well be necessary. There is no comfort in such cases other than remembering that this kind of semi-emergency is often a normal part of the process; all researchers, from students to professionals, know that research projects adapt themselves unwillingly to due dates and that inconveniences do occur.

From the point of completed research to writing, the process is much like that of essay writing (discussed in Chapter 5). You will need an outline, some kind of visual representation of the organization of your paper. The ordering and presentation of your premises, evidence, and conclusions, so that everything follows smoothly without causing doubt or giving pause, require time and reflection, and probably experimentation with more than one arrangement.

From here, it is a matter of *Sitzfleisch*, the padding on your coccyx bone. Good writing results not only from attention to the basics—preparation, outline, knowledge of readership, and the stylistic elements we discuss in Chapter 8—but also from *revising*, the process of repeatedly reading your own writing, learning to identify and improve wordy passages, unclear transitions, and other faults. The usual advice applies: write doggedly; if you get hung up, go on to something else; do not finish the opening and concluding paragraphs until the rest of the paper is done. Above all, *tell your story*. No amount of pseudo-academic writing will save a research paper in which the author has lost interest, or in which the research process was wrongly or incompletely carried out.

On Being Derivative

Many students and other fledgling authors fear being derivative, or basing their entire papers on others' research. But early in a research career (an undergraduate research paper is about as early as it is possible to be) one does not have much experience to draw on. The research process happens from the ground up: background and specifics have to be acquired as part of this process. (If you continue doing projects in a particular field, you will be building on previously acquired knowledge, and you will not have to keep starting anew.) Your first research papers must therefore be based largely on the work of others, primarily or exclusively on secondary sources. Nothing is wrong with this; solid experience using secondary sources is a prerequisite for being able to do primary research.

WHOSE IDEAS?

You may wonder how one can pass off research based on the work of others as one's own. Keep these points in mind:

- *You* chose which sources to use.
- *You* have thoroughly assimilated the material from these sources and paraphrased and reworded to the point that there is no possibility of plagiarism.
- The conclusions *you* drew from these sources are your own.

Choice of Sources

In choosing certain sources over others, trusting one perspective rather than another (sometimes called "privileging"), researchers make decisions for which they can and should be held responsible. That is, were someone to ask why the judgment found in one source was preferred to that found in another, the writer of the research paper should be able to provide an answer. What seems to be "merely" a presentation of information culled from other sources is therefore far more than that; the author, in choosing the sources and deciding what information to consider relevant from each, has shaped the study and made it something unique, not merely a rehash.

The Opening Paragraph

Writing the first paragraph of a research paper is the part of the process that almost always causes the most worry, rewriting, and frustration (not to mention rage). There is no way to avoid some share of this universal experience, so expect it and steel yourself to it. One idea that will always help is to *remember your subject and the points you want to make so you can begin by setting it all up.* Map out a strategy for getting from the general (say, rock music of the 1970s) to the specific (disco, or the punk band you want to talk about, or the emergence of country rock, or anything else). Regardless of what you were taught in high school, *do not* begin conversationally. Introductory passages such as "One of the main reasons I became a music major . . ." or "When I was given this assignment, I first thought I would . . ." tell the reader one thing: the author is having difficulties concentrating and the reader is paying the price—a bad message to send. Rather, *get down to the subject at hand!* Keep creative writing in the background as much as possible.

Conclusions

The end of a research paper must not only follow logically from the coherent presentation of evidence and argument, but also demonstrate understanding and mastery of the subject of the paper. It is impossible to do this—to conclude, summarize, tie up in a neat package—without stating some kind of opinion.

Here is the concluding paragraph from a student research paper, "Folk Songs in the Music of Ralph Vaughan Williams," by Matthew Larson. The paper goes into some detail regarding Vaughan Williams's folk song collecting activities, his lifelong love of the folk idiom, and the ways in which he used both actual folk songs and more general elements from the English musical language—melodic modes, altered scale degrees, melodies that emphasize first and fifth scale degrees, and so on. In conclusion, Mr. Larson writes:

> Vaughan Williams once quoted Gilbert Murray as saying, "The original genius is at once the child of tradition and a rebel against it."[7] Williams himself was both a child of the cosmopolitan musical tradition he was born into and a rebel against it. His dedication to producing uniquely English music, his thorough knowledge of foreign music, and his loyalty to his own art made him the father of the twentieth-century school of composition in England. "He recreated an English musical vernacular, thereby enabling the next generation to take their nationality for granted . . ."[8] The next generation of English composers, even though they rebelled against it, could not help but be influenced and satisfied by the music Vaughan Williams revived. Without his work, English music

[7][Larson's note] Ralph Vaughan Williams, *The Making of Music* (New York: Cornell University Press, 1955), 52.
[8][Larson's note] Hugh Ottaway, "Vaughan Williams, Ralph," *The New Grove Dictionary of Music and Musicians* (London: Macmillan, 1980), vol. 19, 577.

would be nothing more than a hodgepodge of quotations from the music of other nations.

The wording here is rather strong; a couple of things are said that might better not have been. "Quotations" is the wrong word, and it is a bit insulting to suggest that the absence of any one individual would have resulted in a nation's music being a "hodgepodge." (The author might have done better without the last sentence entirely.) But for our purposes, this is beside the point. Mr. Larson has summarized what he wants the reader to take from his presentation of evidence—that Ralph Vaughan Williams's use of folk songs and of individual musical elements therefrom changed the character of English music for the entire century. He presents this not as fact but as his opinion, based on his evaluation of the music and sources he examined. His use of quoted material for context and to strengthen his point is effective and elegant. His conclusions are thus wholly appropriate for a research paper.

Concluding a paper properly is a real challenge, and it is too easy to fall back on certain clichés that are both meaningless and, in terms of the paper's overall effect, destructive. One often-used type of conclusion refuses to take a stand, instead calling for further research. The motivations for this sort of non-opinion are obvious, and they are not always wrong: caution in taking too risky a stand, or humility in not wanting to consider one's own research effort as the last word on a subject. Still, imagine reading, at the end of a substantial, data-driven study: "But it must be stressed that these results are only preliminary, and that they must be taken as such until further research replicates and corroborates these results." The researcher wants to communicate that he or she understands proper research method, that all the problems in the field will not be solved by this single paper, that certain kinds of results need to be reproducible. These cautions are responsible and laudable. However, the message communicated by such a statement drastically weakens the overall impression made by the research—it undermines the entire paper that led to it, and implies that the reader's time would have been better spent another way.

Another strategy consists of what I call "the-future-remains-to-be-seen" conclusions. A sentence such as "Only the future will tell if atonal music will gain ascendancy or if tonality will stage a comeback" is ultimately unhelpful in that it suggests nothing more than a shrug of the author's shoulders. Further, in the vague statement of an oppositional possibility, such conclusions mask deeper and more interesting possibilities that might merit discussion—in this case, say, the yet unimagined musical possibilities that are neither tonal nor atonal, or the coexistence of tonal and atonal music (which is what we currently enjoy). The kind of conclusion parodied above provides one thing: an excuse for a not-too-graceful exit, which is always something to avoid.

Yet another ineffective idea is the quantum-leap summation, "in conclusion, this music was so influential that it led, ultimately, to the music of today" or "this music is so great it will survive eternally." Conclusions of this sort indicate two things: (1) the author has no idea what a conclusion ought to be, and (2) he or she at least wants to acknowledge that the music is important, somehow. These, too, are utterly insufficient conclusions.

The best way to approach conclusions, when one is having difficulty wrapping up, is to reread the paper several times (always a good idea in any case) in order to recapture a *global* sense of where it has been leading. Firm conclusions based on that, even if highly personal ("All this documentary material leads me to believe . . ."), are always more persuasive than an unwillingness to take any position at all, or a plaintive call for further research. Particularly on the undergraduate level, the paper may well be leading toward an assertion about which there is little disagreement—"It seems clear that Brahms's love of historical music was a strong influence on his choral compositions"—but such conclusions have presumably been prepared and backed up by the paper itself and are therefore sufficiently strong and appropriate.

Returning to Mr. Larson's conclusions, we note again how "authorial" they are, how they represent a personal position that results from the information presented. Larson's conclusion nicely illustrates a central point: no matter how extensively other sources have been used in a music research paper, it remains a very personal and subjective kind of project, and the author is not only present but responsible for the sources chosen and examined and the conclusions drawn. The responsibilities are great; because many skills are necessary in assembling a persuasive, informative presentation of research, research projects are among the most work-intensive writing projects in the musical field. When mastered, though, these skills prove useful in all areas of endeavor.

7

A SAMPLE RESEARCH PAPER IN MUSIC

On the following pages is a research paper by Amie Margoles, who was a first-year undergraduate student in horn performance at the time she wrote it. The paper, "Gershwin's French Connection," examines the question of French influence in Gershwin's music (*An American in Paris* in particular) and the relative importance of his visits to Paris and awareness of contemporary trends in French music. Note the use of musical examples, quotations, and citations; this presentation is a fine model for the use of scholarly apparatus.

Amie Margoles
Dr. Bellman
MUS 152
May 2, 1997

Gershwin's French Connection

In biographies and articles on George Gershwin (1898–1937), references to Paris and French composers, particularly Ravel and Debussy, arise many times. It is evident that the music of French Impressionist composers and possibly France itself, either directly or indirectly, influences some of Gershwin's music. According to pianist Frances Veri, to play his music "One has to recognize when

he is being Gershwin the American, and when he is being
Gershwin the Frenchman."[1]

In his lifetime, Gershwin made two trips to Paris, the first in
1923 and the second in 1928. On the first trip he was taken in tow
by dapper *boulevardier* and Cartier executive Jules Glaenzer.
Glaenzer was best known for hosting glittering parties for international society at his apartments in both New York and Paris. Having
befriended Gershwin in 1921, Glaenzer mainly considered him a
bright talent who could amuse and entertain his (Glaenzer's)
wealthy and celebrated friends and clients. At this time Gershwin
was already a popular songwriter (best known for "Swanee"), and
he was a talented and entertaining pianist. There was a saying
around New York that it wasn't difficult to persuade Gershwin to
play the piano, it was difficult to persuade Gershwin to *not* play the
piano.[2] Glaenzer's *soirees* were not just social; they were an opportunity to sell jewelry to wealthy guests. A celebrated pal like
Gershwin, who was always eager to entertain, usually assured a
big turn-out.[3]

Besides introducing Gershwin to society, Glaenzer gave himself credit for having groomed several entertainers for celebrity
and stardom. Glaenzer asserted, without hesitation, that Gershwin
was his "best pupil."[4] This was probably true, since under
Glaenzer's tutelage, Gershwin had begun to (occasionally) remove
his ever-present cigar when he was speaking face-to-face with
young ladies. Also with Glaenzer's influence, Gershwin made

[1]Stuart Isacoff, "Fascinatin' Gershwin," *Keyboard Classics* 4/1 (January-February
1984), 8.
[2]Edward Jablonski, "George Gershwin at the Keyboard," *Keyboard Classics* 3
(November-December 1993), 12.
[3]Edward Jablonski, *Gershwin* (New York: Doubleday, 1987), 56.
[4]Alan Kendall, *George Gershwin* (New York: University Books, 1987), 34.

other adjustments in his etiquette and, although his wardrobe was already natty, he sharpened it up even more.[5]

In the same manner that Glaenzer had introduced Gershwin to the socially elite, he set out to introduce Gershwin to Paris. It could not have been an ordinary visit, given Glaenzer's propensity for style and dash. Glaenzer went all out to assure a memorable time and it was April, the most beautiful time in the city. Gershwin and his lyricist, G. D. ("Buddy") DeSylva, were taken to the swank restaurants and to the exciting cabarets and nightspots. They cruised the boulevards, and there is a story that, on this visit, as he rode through the city in a cab, Gershwin turned to DeSylva and exclaimed, "Why, this is a city you can write about!" DeSylva answered, "Don't look now, George, but it's been done."[6]

According to Gershwin biographer Alan Kendall, Gershwin lacked what was then considered a basic education. This lacking caused him to miss much of what European culture had to offer, but it also enabled him to respond directly to stimuli. "There was something refreshing and reassuring about his naiveté, as there still can be in Americans in their first encounter with new experiences . . . the fact that he wrote a piece entitled *An American in Paris* . . . had a great deal [to do] with how he saw [Paris], from an American point of view."[7]

Gershwin biographer Charles Schwartz also sees a connection between Gershwin's visits to Paris and *An American in Paris*. Schwartz writes that Gershwin's first visit to Paris likely provided the stimuli for the piece and that "if *An American in Paris* was triggered by his 1923 springtime adventure in France, it was further stimulated

---

[5]Charles Schwartz, *Gershwin: His Life and Music* (Indianapolis: Bobbs-Merrill, 1973), 48.
[6]Kendall, 81.
[7]Ibid., 82.

by a visit he made to Paris, later, in 1928."[8] Schwartz believes that Gershwin went back to Paris, specifically to study and to work on *An American in Paris,* which was then a work in progress, citing an interview of Gershwin carried by the journal *Musical America* (February 18, 1928) in which Gershwin stated that he wanted "to work on an orchestral ballet, *An American in Paris,* while abroad[,] and to study."[9]

Gershwin biographer Edward Jablonski has another view of Gershwin's second trip to Paris. He writes, "before he set out for Europe, Gershwin had blocked out the work quite thoroughly, so that, despite musicological legend, he didn't go to Paris to write *An American in Paris*; it was virtually complete, except for orchestration, before he sailed from Manhattan . . . Gershwin had told writer-artist Charles G. Shaw that he loved Paris for its beauty, London for its calm, and New York as the greatest city for work."[10]

However, it seems evident from a letter Gershwin wrote to Mabel Schirmer, that he was planning to study and work in France. As quoted by Jablonski, Gershwin writes: "I expect that we will stay in Paris for about two weeks and then go someplace where the climate is right, and where I can do some work. If, however, I find somebody to study with in Paris, I may take a place on the outskirts and stay there most of the time."[11]

During Gershwin's time, Paris was considered the leading music center of the world, as it had been for several decades. Musicians from all over the world thronged there to visit, to live, and to work.[12] Specifically, Paris was the home of the finest teachers and practitioners of impressionistic and other types of modern music.

[8]Schwartz, 154.
[9]Ibid.
[10]Jablonski, *Gershwin,* 152.
[11]Ibid.
[12]Schwartz, 303.

According to Jablonski, an experience of Gershwin's at about the time he was planning the trip to France may have stimulated his search for a teacher. Jablonski writes that impressionist composer Maurice Ravel had arrived in the United States in January, 1928, to begin a four-month tour. For the celebration of Ravel's 53rd birthday, his hostess in New York, Eva Gautier, asked if he had any special requests. Ravel told her that he wished to meet George Gershwin and to see some of his musicals. At the birthday dinner, Gershwin played *Rhapsody in Blue* and his entire repertoire. Gautier is quoted as saying, "the thing that astonished Ravel was the facility with which George scaled the most formidable technical difficulties and his genius for weaving complicated rhythms and his gift for melody."[13]

Gautier acted as interpreter and, through her, Gershwin told Ravel that he wished to study with him. Jablonski writes, "As Gautier remembered it, Ravel told Gershwin that he did not think it was a good idea. Ravel expressed to Gershwin that lessons would probably cause Gershwin to write 'bad Ravel' and diminish his gift of melody and spontaneity. Instead, Ravel provided Gershwin with a letter of introduction to the renowned French teacher, Nadia Boulanger."[14]

When the Gershwin entourage, consisting of George, his brother Ira, their sister Frances, and Ira's wife Leonore arrived in Paris on March 25, 1928, they were greeted by Mabel and Bob Schirmer, close friends since George's Tin Pan Alley days, and by Joseph Rosanska, who was then concertizing in Europe. They settled into the Hotel Majestic, where they stayed, with the exception of a couple of side excursions, until leaving for America in early June. Gershwin had a Steinway piano moved into his room,

---

[13]Jablonski, *Gershwin,* 154.
[14]Ibid., 152.

unpacked his *American in Paris* sketches, music paper, and reference books. He excitedly showed Mabel Schirmer the letter from Ravel to Boulanger and asked her to accompany him when he presented it to the great teacher.[15]

Meeting Boulanger seemed to be of primary importance to Gershwin, since it was one of the first matters in which he expressed immediate interest. Many celebrated composers had studied (or would study) with Mlle. Boulanger, including Aaron Copland, Virgil Thomson, Walter Piston, Roy Harris, and David Diamond. Gershwin, who didn't know that Boulanger spoke English, took Mabel Schirmer along for his interview, to help interpret and, possibly, to provide the moral support one derives from a close friend. Although Boulanger was aware of Gershwin and his success, after hearing him play she concurred with Ravel. She expressed admiration for Gershwin's style, but she felt that he would not benefit from her instruction. It is possible that Gershwin interpreted this to mean that she believed she had nothing more to contribute and, although rejected, he felt mildly flattered. Nevertheless, he took the rejection well, and did not seem overly chagrined.[16]

Gershwin's meeting with Boulanger has been subject to controversy since, according to Kendall, it has been suggested that Gershwin was rejected because the great teacher didn't think much of his musicianship and promise as a student—not worth the waste of her valuable time. On many occasions, Boulanger has denied that she doubted Gershwin's ability to cope with an intense course of study, although other authorities believe that Gershwin would not have responded well to her arduous style.[17] Boulanger remained

---

[15]Ibid., 157.
[16]Kendall, 84.
[17]Ibid.

reticent on the issue, particularly after Gershwin's death. However, she is reported to have said, "It is never wise to enter a tunnel, unless there is a good chance of coming out on the other side."[18]

Most important for Gershwin during his stay in Paris were the many contacts he had with leading musicians. Among others, he met with Serge Prokofiev, Darius Milhaud, William Walton, Francis Poulenc, Leopold Stokowski, Alexandre Tansman, Georges Auric, Jacques Ibert, and Vittorio Rieti. At every opportunity, Gershwin would play his music and, with few exceptions (Prokofiev being one), they all responded favorably and encouraged him in his work. Stokowski even volunteered to conduct the premiere of *An American in Paris* before learning that Damrosch had already put in his bid for the composition.[19]

Gershwin also enlisted Mabel Schirmer in the task of helping him find some taxi horns. He felt that these horns suffused Paris with one of its most indigenous sounds, and wished to incorporate them into *An American in Paris*. She obliged by taking him to several auto supply shops in the Grand Armée. "As Schirmer translated, Gershwin squeezed until he could find horns with the 'honk' and 'squawk' that suited his purpose; some were wonderfully off-key. Gershwin purchased several which they took back to the Majestic."[20]

The presence of these "instruments" in Gershwin's hotel room led to a memorable episode for two Paris Conservatory students, Jacques Fray and Mario Braggiotti. They were both piano students who had an admiration for the two-piano arrangement of *Rhapsody in Blue*. Hoping to meet their hero, they rang the bell of Gershwin's room and, evidently, interrupted his work. As quoted by Jablonski, Braggiotti later wrote that Gershwin ushered them into his room

[18]Schwartz, 128.
[19]Ibid., 156.
[20]Jablonski,*Gershwin,* 158.

"with that vague and stunned manner of one who is holding tightly to the thread of a creative mood."[21] Nothing was said, then, suddenly, Gershwin went to the piano, "sat in front of his manuscripts and quickly finished a musical sentence that my bell ringing had interrupted."[22]

Jablonski writes, "Gershwin then stood and noticed his guests staring at the taxi horn collection lying on a card table. 'I'm looking for the right horn pitch for a street scene for a ballet I'm writing,' he told them. 'Calling it *An American in Paris* . . . lots of fun. I think I've got something. Just finished sketching the slow movement' . . . Gesturing to Braggiotti, he said 'Here, I want to try this accompaniment. Won't you play the melody in the treble?' "[23] As described by Jablonski, Braggiotti moved swiftly beside Gershwin at the piano. Gershwin began the two-bar vamp and Braggiotti joined in, reading the single note lead from the fresh manuscript. "For the first time anywhere, there echoed the amazingly original and nostalgic slow movement of *An American in Paris*, undoubtedly one of Gershwin's most brilliant works."[24]

These young musicians also experienced, first-hand, Gershwin's use for the taxi horns. He explained that he hoped to evoke the sound of the Parisian traffic by using real taxi horns in his "ballet." "He conscripted the two young men as 'hornists,' turned to the opening of the piece and played it, cueing them on their parts with a nod."[25]

The musical responsiveness of these two young students evidently impressed Gershwin. After that audaciously impromptu meeting, Gershwin accompanied Braggiotti and Fray back to

[21]Ibid., 159.
[22]Ibid.
[23]Ibid.
[24]Ibid., 160.
[25]Ibid.

Fray's flat to hear them play Fray's unique twin-keyboard piano, a Pleyel.[26] For their help, Gershwin offered them positions in *Funny Face* and when they later came to the United States as the two-piano team of Braggiotti and Fray, making their debut in Carnegie Hall, Gershwin was a helpful champion and friend.[27]

When not socializing or discussing music with fellow musicians and composers, Gershwin managed to get into the streets of Paris to absorb ambiance. He and Ira strolled throughout the city, they had their coffee at the sidewalk restaurants, they climbed the Eiffel Tower, where George had his portrait sketched, and they attended some concerts of the local, and often awkward, versions of *Rhapsody in Blue*.[28] Gershwin also stopped at every music house in Paris that owned an original work by Debussy until he had purchased the composer's complete collection.[29] He also continued work on the piano version of *An American in Paris*.[30]

During one of Gershwin's social engagements, he encountered Stravinsky at the home of the violinist Paul Kochanski. Gershwin could not let the opportunity slip and, from that, a famous exchange occurred in front of at least one witness, composer Richard Hammond. Gershwin, still seeking lessons in the impressionist method, told Stravinsky that he wished to study with him. "The Russian—now *très parisien*—composer looked up and inquired, 'How much money do you make [a year], Mr. Gershwin?' Off guard, Gershwin told him a sum that ran into six figures. 'In that case,' Stravinsky told him, 'I should study with you.' That characteristic quip terminated Gershwin's quest for a teacher in Paris."[31]

[26]Ibid.
[27]Ibid.
[28]Ibid., 161.
[29]Isacoff, 9.
[30]Jablonski, *Gershwin,* 168.
[31]Ibid.

In late June of 1928, when Gershwin returned to New York, he packed his most treasured mementos from Paris: four French taxi horns, eight handsome leather-bound volumes of Debussy's complete works, and a French Mostel reed organ, which he had installed in his studio and on which he occasionally played.[32]

On November 18, 1928, orchestration for *An American in Paris* was completed. The pre-orchestration sketch itself, written mostly on three and four staves, as one would a two-piano version of the piece, had been completed several months earlier, on August 1.[33] Schwartz quotes the August 18, 1928 issue of *Musical America,* in which Gershwin says the following:

> This new piece, really a rhapsodic ballet, is written very freely and is the most modern music I've yet attempted. The opening part will be developed in typical French style, in the manner of Debussy and the Six, though the tunes are all original. My purpose here is to portray the impressions of an American visitor in Paris as he strolls about the city, listens to the various street noises, and absorbs the French atmosphere. As in my other orchestral compositions, I've not endeavored to present any definite scenes in this music. The rhapsody is programmatic only in a general impressionistic way, so that the individual listener can read into the music such episodes as his imagination pictures for him.[34]

---

[32]Schwartz, 159.
[33]Ibid., 164.
[34]Ibid. Schwartz also notes Gershwin's evident lack of "savvy," due to his grouping of Debussy with *Les Six,* as the styles and musical philosophies of the latter attempted to be antithetical to impressionism and every other type of musical style. However, Gershwin may have intended to combine elements of both schools, considering all of it to be "French."

As noted earlier, Gershwin wasn't so much influenced by Paris as he allowed Paris to provide a background for a uniquely American response, although *An American in Paris* conveys much of the character, romance, and stimulation of Paris in the earlier part of the twentieth century. However, the greatest French quality reflected in Gershwin's work is the thread of French style, particularly impressionism, which passes through many of his pieces.

Impressionism is a term which originally described the work of a group of French artists, particularly Degas, Renoir, Monet, and Manet, who were active in the last three decades of the nineteenth century. Their work is characterized by the subtle play of light and shadow, rather than the clear definition of specific objects. Impressionism has also been applied to the musical composition of Claude Debussy (1862–1918)—who objected to the term—and to the works of Maurice Ravel (1875–1937), and others composing between 1890 and 1915.[35]

Impressionistic music expressed the reaction against form and styles such as clear sonata forms, fugues, canonic imitation, and the characteristics of Wagnerian opera. According to Evan Copley, "viewed from the vantage point of history, the impressionistic movement seems more like a final French nationalistic Romanticism, although the movement influenced Stravinsky, Delius, and many others. The intent is to suggest a mood and to evoke an atmosphere through the avoidance of clearly defined forms and statements."[36] This description seems consistent with Gershwin's stated intention for *An American in Paris,* in which the composer endeavored to avoid definite scenes and simply wished to suggest

---

[35]R. Evan Copley, *Harmony: Baroque to Contemporary,* vol. 2 (Champaign, IL: Stipes, 1991), 78.
[36]Ibid.

an atmosphere, allowing the individual listener to construct his own forms.

According to Michael Tilson Thomas, Gershwin made a great study of Debussy and Ravel. Thomas asserts that Gershwin was a serious student, continually working, maturing, and expanding.[37] In *An American in Paris,* it was clearly Gershwin's intention to be taken seriously. He had hoped that his time in France, then the center of modern concert music, would help to broaden his own musical technique. Gershwin believed that "a tone poem, suitable for ballet, would place him in the company of the most *au courant* of French composers and the adoptive Parisian, Stravinsky."[38] In regard to *An American in Paris,* Steven Gilbert writes,

> A solo by the English horn dreamily recalls the main theme . . . whereas, [later in the piece] parallel chords sound out the first six notes of the main theme 1. [Example 7.1] Harmonically, these two excerpts contain some of the most inspired writing in the entire work, and they readily reveal the source of the inspiration . . . with its wash of diatonic dissonance, this recasting of the main theme 1 is the most French-sounding of the piece; at the same time, the not-incompatible influence of Stravinsky can be seen in the un-Gershwinesque pattern of changing meters.[39]

In regard to another excerpt from *An American in Paris,* Gilbert points out that the verticals are in parallel motion in all voices. He adds, "The melody is diatonic, the verticals are not.

---

[37]Isacoff, 8.
[38]Steven E. Gilbert, *The Music of Gershwin* (New Haven: Yale University Press, 1995), 90.
[39]Ibid., 120.

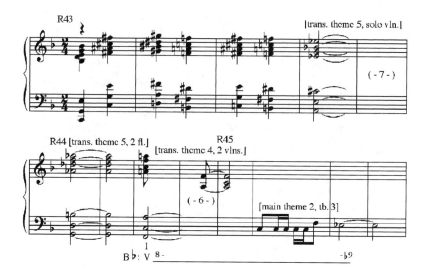

EX. 7.1

Gershwin, *An American in Paris,* transition to section 3 (condensed).

Their structure is the same harmony that Stravinsky made famous in the so-called 'Petroushka chord,' and one to which Gershwin would eventually return in *Porgy and Bess*."[40]

Isacoff writes that French influences abound in works such as the *I Got Rhythm Variations,* "where gentle pentatonic arpeggios in Gershwin find their counterpart in works like Debussy's *Suite Bergamasque*."[41] (See Example 7.2.) According to Isacoff, Gershwin's propensity for patterns and fast-moving repeated notes or chords can also be considered an impressionistic feature of his writing.[42]

[40]Ibid., 121.
[41]Isacoff, 9.
[42]Ibid., 10. Isacoff also writes: "This aspect of keyboard style can be linked as well to the American novelty tradition, exemplified by the compositions of Zez Confrey ('Kitten on the Keys') and John Alden Carpenter (*Krazy Kat*)."

EX. 7.2a
Gershwin, *I Got Rhythm Variations,* transition to the first variation.

EX. 7.2b
Debussy, *Suite Bergamasque,* Prelude, opening.

According to Copley, the use of pentatonic scales, irregular
and frequently static harmonic rhythms, and parallel seventh
chords and triads are specific harmonic techniques characterizing
impressionism[43]—all characteristics Steven Gilbert identifies in *An
American in Paris.*[44] Gilbert writes that pentatonicism also played
an important role in Gershwin's music almost from the beginning,

[43]Copley, 78.
[44]Gilbert, 121.

EX. 7.3

Gershwin, "They All Laughed," opening.

particularly plagal melodies which operated "from the fourth below the tonic to the fifth above."[45] He cites examples of Gershwin's
plagal pentatonicism in the refrain melodies of "Clap Yo' Hands"
and "Maybe." According to Gilbert, the plagal pentatonicism characterized in "They All Laughed" (Example 7.3), written in 1937, is a
strong reminder that Gershwin never abandoned this impressionistic element of his earlier styles.[46]

It wasn't simply Gershwin's visits to Paris that stimulated his interest in impressionistic techniques. The techniques and harmonies
of Debussy, Ravel and others had, by Gershwin's time, found their
way into American art music and into the popular mainstream.[47]
Gershwin had already been introduced to Debussy by his teacher,
Charles Hambitzer, with whom he had studied from age fourteen

---

[45]Ibid., 148.

[46]Ibid., 217.

[47]Isacoff, 9. "In turn," Isacoff writes, "European composers became fascinated by America's blues and ragtime. Thus, Milhaud produced *The Creation of the World,* Stravinsky composed *Ragtime*; Ravel, after a trip to America in 1922, wrote the opera *L'Enfant et les sortilèges,* in which a teapot sings 'Tea for Two' to a cup."

to about eighteen. There is evidence that Gershwin was a serious student, as he credits Hambitzer with making him "harmony conscious and, although Gershwin continued to play his own work for the pleasure of his friends and in concert, he often turned to the music of others for pleasure and study."[48]

Artis Wodehouse has written that Gershwin's music was a product of lively, highly evolved idioms that were developed as Gershwin was musically coming of age. According to Wodehouse, the most significant idiom of Gershwin's early years was the piano roll song arrangement (from 1916 to 1926, Gershwin cut approximately 120 piano rolls). Wodehouse believes that one can "glimpse the broad range of vernacular and high culture musical styles" that Gershwin could call upon in "his growing mastery of the particular harmonic vocabulary that would prove to be the hallmark of his mature music."[49]

Wodehouse states further:

> In the case of Gershwin's own roll arrangement of "So Am I," the composer has seized upon those [musical] implications that relate to the vocabulary of French Impressionism and late nineteenth century harmony: parallel chords, root movement of chords by thirds, ambivalence of major and minor, chords of the ninth, and pentatonic scale. The break materials of the piece are based upon these chords, scales, and harmonic progressions. By taking all of the materials of the piece from the melody, it becomes possible to design a climactic structure which peaks after the

[48]Jablonski, "George Gershwin at the Keyboard," 11.
[49]Artis Wodehouse, "George Gershwin: The Missing Years," *Keyboard Classics* 10/1 (January-February 1990), 6.

blues break of measures 63–64, and comes to
rest after an extended dreamy coda which features
pentatonic fragments taken from previous break
material.[50]

Elsewhere, Wodehouse explains how Gershwin, in the decep-
tively simple melodies of "'S Wonderful" and "Funny Face" in
1928, crafted work of soaring scope. This was achieved by setting
them in an antiphonal call-and-response pattern against a more
complex momentum-producing motive. Wodehouse writes:

[Gershwin] passes this call-and-response pattern
through a sophisticated harmonic progression using the
harmonies developed by Debussy and Ravel in such a
way that the initial verse melody refuses to come to
harmonic rest until the first presentation of the "'S Wonderful" chorus.[51]

In a survey of Gershwin's life and in the complete range of
music that he composed, it is clear that impressionism and other
French-based styles are a thread running though his compositions.
They are not, however, the major influences on Gershwin's writing.
Ragtime, blues, klezmer, and Gershwin's own melodic creativity
are evident in his works and have been acknowledged and described by Gershwin scholars. Certainly France did not create
Gershwin's style, but it did provide a backdrop that most likely inspired one of his finest compositions, *An American in Paris*. For
Gershwin, France was primarily a place from which important
work in modern music was emerging. It drew Gershwin, who was
described by Michael Tilson Thomas as an "immense student,"

---

[50]Ibid., 6.
[51]Artis Wodehouse, "The Undiscovered Gershwin: His Solo Piano Improvisations,"
Keyboard Classics 7/6 (November-December 1987), 10.

continually working, maturing, and expanding his conceptions. Gershwin evidently admired and studied the work of Debussy, but with or without the help of the impressionists and others, Gershwin would apply all that he could learn around him and all that he could discover within himself. In the judgment of many musicologists, Gershwin is the greatest American composer. He is, however, an American composer with a French connection.

COMMENTARY ON THE MARGOLES PAPER

This paper addresses the question of how to square the quintessentially American Gershwin with a French aesthetic, interest, and possible influence. At first glance, the answer seems obvious from the title of the tone poem *An American in Paris,* which followed the second of the composer's two voyages to that city; the usual story is that he composed out his impressions of a foreign capital. The real answer, though, is somewhat more complicated, and involves not only Gershwin's travels, but also his previous musical interests, his professional aspirations, and most interestingly the extent to which American music had already assimilated French influences by the 1920s. To provide a full answer, Ms. Margoles adopts an organizational format that incorporates both chronological and topical approaches.

She begins with a pithy statement of the issue: how French is the music of the American Gershwin? Only a short paragraph is needed. From here she can proceed to the most immediate background: narratives of Gershwin's trips to Paris and the genesis of *An American in Paris.* Perhaps because of the involved nature of this narrative (travelogue, famous anecdote about taxi horns, stories of Gershwin's frustrated attempts to secure a high-profile composition teacher), it is in this section that two small oversights occur. First, Gershwin's friend Mabel Schirmer is only introduced to us at her second appearance; the first time, her name appears without explanation. Second, Gershwin's attempts to study with Maurice Ravel and Nadia Boulanger are separated from his attempt to study with Igor Stravinsky by the lengthy and very different anecdote about the taxi horns and the Jacques Fray/Mario Braggiotti piano duo. The structure and coherence would have been better served by having the Ravel, Boulanger, and Stravinsky anecdotes next to each other, making a tight little subsection with a clear ending ("That characteristic quip terminated Gershwin's quest for a teacher in Paris").

Chronology and personal connections established, though, Margoles can move on to deeper considerations. She changes focus with an artful transition that uses a quote from Gershwin himself, ". . . developed in typical French style, in the manner of Debussy and the Six." After a helpful clarifying footnote, she can proceed to a discussion of the kinds of musical elements the composer was probably referring to with the designation "impressionism," which includes a quotation from the analytical literature and some musical examples showing parallel chords and pentatonicism. Finally, she can return full circle to the United States, pointing out that these elements had already been present in American music—art music and popular music both—whether via French influence or not. Thus, Gershwin's musical "French Connection" (that phrase being a play on the title of a popular film of 1971, obviously) is shown to be something less simple than it first appears. The paper is a wholly successful presentation, supported by fine scholarly apparatus (citations of a variety of different sources, including well-deployed quotations) and excellent writing.

Note that the successful use of sources involves more than just looking at lots of them, or citing them properly; a wide variety of material must be internalized and the necessary information gleaned from it to enable the author to tell his or her story (as opposed to the sources' stories). This information is then presented, as part of the author's narrative, in a congenial mixture of paraphrase and direct quotation (of course, fully cited throughout). In the final paper, all the important elements of good research need to be present: a coherent story to tell, more than enough source material to back it up, and engaging, readable presentation from the perspective of both writing and source citation. This paper exemplifies the kind of undergraduate research that is possible with time and persistence (and that deserves to be seen by more than one reader).

8

STYLE IN WRITING

"I quite agree with you," said the Duchess; "and the moral of that is—'Be what you would seem to be'—or if you'd like it put more simply—'Never imagine yourself not to be otherwise than what it might appear to others that what you were or might have been was not otherwise than what you had been would have appeared to them to be otherwise.'"

"I think I should understand that better," Alice said very politely, "if I had it written down."

—LEWIS CARROLL, *ALICE IN WONDERLAND*

THE MEANING OF "STYLE"

Style in writing consists of those aspects that make each author's writing individual. When, as a reader, you sense that an author is heavy-handed, elegant, terse, animated, or bland, you are thinking about matters of style. Style encompasses choices regarding vocabulary (for example, "pleased" vs. "ecstatic"), syntax (sentence structure, complexity, and length), and even the general musicality of the prose. Style will also reflect the tone, which is closely bound up with both the author's position and the audience he or she seeks to reach. Through style choices, the author projects a certain mood and affect (in addition to communicating information), thereby telling us something about himself or herself.

Examples of writing style intended for a broad readership are to be found in Chapters 2 and 4. Now, since a great deal of writing about music is intended for an academic or at least academically trained readership, let us focus more closely on that variety. Here are two contrasting passages, both rich in content and lively in style, written by academics with primarily academic audiences in mind. We begin with Alejandro E. Planchart's summary of the structure and content of a section of the closing *Agnus Dei* of a Renaissance mass, the *Missa Ave Regina Celorum* of Guillaume Du Fay:

> The triplet section, with its dance-like rhythms, and particularly with its sudden stop and resumption, is indeed at once an image of a round dance and, in the brilliance of its sound, also of the *visio beatifica,* a passage of enormous power that only one who would have read Dante's *Commedia* could imagine. The connection of the round-dance and the *visio beatifica* had, throughout the middle ages, a fixed point of linguistic reference, in that the most common term for the rejoicing of the blessed in heaven was the word *tripudio,* a word found literally in hundreds of hymns, sequences, and other devotional literature, and a word that in normal parlance meant to dance. But there is also a visual version of the combination of round dance and heavenly vision, and that was precisely in the decoration of the cupolas of Italian churches, built from the early *quattrocento* onwards; so in a sense the final Agnus in the mass is a recollection of a place like Santa Maria del Fiore. The final Agnus is a fitting end to a work that remains, as Fallows has correctly remarked, 'a bursting cornucopia of musical invention'. . . [1]

A general reader is usually not, of course, expected to be conversant with the Beatific Vision as found in Dante's *Divine Comedy* (titles are normally given in the original language), the stop-and-start nature of Renaissance round dances, and the paintings that animate cathedral domes. A reader with a minimum of patience and some small exposure to Western civilization, though, can understand this passage without any problem; after all, the one Latin word with no clear English cognate (*tripudio*) is translated and explained. (Discussion of the use of the Italian word *quattrocento* will follow below, under Obscure Words.) What is abundantly clear in the passage is the way this music springs from the culture that produced it—from popular dance to literary imagery to visual imagery to theology—and moreover the author's exultation in the music and everything associated with it. The quotation of another scholar's words at the end of the passage is the sort of thing that nonacademic readers often dislike, but is completely appropriate here; another's eloquent phrase, duly credited, serves to support and cap one's own elucidation of a particular point. The sum total is a passage of great learning that is also lively and suggestive, all because of choices made pertaining to style.

(A short aside, here: the use of others' words with correct credit given is often found by nonacademics to be intimidating and pretentious. To that, I can only say that many people are intimidated far too easily! Academics usually want to use the most effective and accurate turns of phrase—nothing at all wrong with this—and to give credit where it is due rather than wrongly taking credit themselves, which is the ethical position. Absolutely no apology or self-consciousness for this practice is necessary.)

We find a different but no less lively approach in this passage by James Parakilas, which discusses key elements of French musical hispanicism:

> What evidently caught Debussy's ear in Ravel's Habanera is that Ravel takes the stock elements of the genre and, by inverting them, liberates them in function. That is, he turns the stock triplet-to-duplet-eighth rhythm of habanera melodies . . . into a bass rhythm, and the stock bass rhythm . . . into a melodic rhythm. [Example 8.1] Then he switches back and forth between the stock arrangement and the inverted one, and in so doing he makes each rhythm an independent element, not tied to any one function, either conventional or unconventional. And Ravel gives these elements, these rhythms, not only independence of function, but independence from each other in harmony and in timing (the melodic elements entering unpredictably against the ostinato pattern). . . .

EX. 8.1
Maurice Ravel, *Sites auriculaires,* "Habanera," opening.

Debussy made this transformation of the habanera a means of evoking a specific Spanish image—a place and an atmosphere long established in the canon of the Spanish exotic: night in the gardens of the Alhambra. His habanera, like Ravel's, is no longer a specific dance but a source of musical elements that float freely through the imagination. Debussy uses it to situate a dreamy persona in a tranquil imagined spot—the Alhambra garden—from where many different Spanish sounds can be "heard": Gypsy music from the streets of Granada far below, Moorish music from the distant past.[2]

We find here a rather sophisticated discussion of individual musical elements—the habanera dance rhythm and the triplet-to-duplet melodic rhythm associated with it—and how their innovative deployment enables a familiar flavor of Spanish exoticism to expand in breadth and aesthetic possibility while remaining no less redolent of fairy-tale Spain. The musical example illustrates the point, so that the various juxtapositions of abstract rhythms may be "heard" with actual pitches. Once this technical matter is explained and illustrated, though, Parakilas can tell us what it *means*, moving from a technical discussion to an evocation of the ancient Spanish fantasyland the music evokes. He uses virtually no musical terminology more specialized than "habanera," but his sentences show a good deal of structural contrast (more on sentence structure shortly). So, because of his exemplary musical ear for prose, he is able to cover a great deal of musical terrain—historical, technical, and cultural—with an unpretentious, grateful literary style.

Both of these passages pass what is perhaps the ultimate test for writing about music: they are so vividly evocative that the reader can almost hear the music described, whether there is an example present or not. The point is worth stressing, since "academic style" is an all-too-common euphemism for "boring." As stated earlier, academic thought merits academic style, but academic style can be as exciting as any other kind, and questions of what constitutes it and when and how to use it deserve consideration. It is not simply a matter of longer sentences for academics vs. shorter sentences for civilians, so to speak, nor is it a matter of twenty-dollar vocabulary vs. one-syllable, two-for-a-quarter words. Rather, it is a matter of the kind of thought an academic audience can be expected to share, and the kind of writing that reflects that thought process.

---

[2]James Parakilas, "How Spain Got a Soul," in Jonathan Bellman, ed., *The Exotic in Western Music* (Boston: Northeastern University Press, 1998), 173–74.

ACADEMIC STYLE TRAITS

Complex Sentence Structure

Characteristics often (rightly or wrongly) associated with academic style include the use of many syllables and words rather than few; the choice to phrase a statement as the inverse of a negative rather than a simple positive ("it is not unlikely that Josquin des Prez studied with Johannes Ockeghem" or "the stirring sound of the Scottish bagpipes is not without a certain rough beauty"); use of an obscure word or one from a foreign language (e.g., *quattrocento*) when a commonplace English word might do as well or better; and relying on mystifyingly complex sentence structure. True, these characteristics can make for difficult reading, and are often better avoided, yet they can also be better than the alternatives. The essence of academic writing is that the full measure of intellectual and conceptual breadth requires the full vocabulary and syntactical resources of the English language for expression. Academic writing certainly carries some risk: at their worst, long and complex sentences do not hold together, and rarefied vocabulary obscures rather than illuminates. These, however, are faults of execution, not intrinsic weaknesses of academic writing per se.

Obscure Words

In the first passage above, Planchart uses the word *quattrocento,* four hundreds, which is an abbreviation for *millequattrocento,* one thousand and four hundreds. The Italian language designates centuries slightly more intuitively than English, so that *trecento* is the 1300s, the *quattrocento* is the 1400s, and so on. (Context indicates whether the *mille* is implied, or if an author is really talking about the fourth or fifth century of the Common Era.) Surely, we wonder, the author might have used "the early fifteenth century" or "the early 1400s" so as to be less elitist, instead of writing only for the (at very least) bilingual? True, he might have, but this is one of those nuances of connotation better served by a foreign term, because the Italian designation for that particular century results in a slightly different emphasis. The implication of *quattrocento* is not "what the Italians were doing to their churches in the early fifteenth century," but rather "the *Italian* fifteenth century," which suggests a specific geography, culture, worldview, school of church decoration, etc., to which Du Fay's music corresponds in the way described: as a musical cognate to religious painting.

This is a fine point but an powerful one, and it would have gone unnoticed had the author simply said "beginning in the early fifteenth century."

Since a foreign word can have its own slight difference of meaning and implication from the English equivalent, therefore, it can be the best style choice. In other situations, though, specialized academic jargon can render a passage all but incomprehensible. Consider a passage in which the editors of a collection of independent but related studies explain that certain of the studies

> offer close readings of authorial subjectivities that reveal the intrasubjective conflicts and fragmentations manifest in dynamics of idealization and denigration, splitting, ambivalence, and denial, as they are experienced in relation to different musical selves or projected onto musical others.[3]

Res ipsa loquitur, as they say in legal circles: the thing speaks for itself. The target audience of such writing is tiny to begin with, even among academics, and there is absolutely no reason not to strive for more clarity. Whatever merit results from using such jargon does not offset the resulting obscurity of the passage.

First Person Plural

One of the (now less common) formulas of academic writing consists of using the corporate first person plural, the so-called "papal we" or "royal we." In many cases, this is an affectation, a bald-faced pretense of objectivity when a subjective opinion is being offered. The difference this single word makes can be great. Compare the differing tone in the following two sentences:

> I tend to view big band jazz as a hybrid popular form.

> We tend to view big band jazz as a hybrid popular form.

The first sentence is a statement of individual opinion, no more threatening than any other, to be evaluated on its merits. This version proclaims, in its use of the first person singular, that it is an opinion, which means that the author is actively taking responsibility for it. The first person plural of the second sentence, though, implies some kind of

---

[3]Georgina Born and David Hesmondhalgh, Introduction to *Western Music and its Others: Difference, Representation, and Appropriation in Music* (Berkeley and Los Angeles, University of California Press, 2000), 33.

consensus of the well-informed and authoritative, and in doing so it allows the author to hide behind this imagined consensus, taking little or no responsibility for the opinion and maintaining a kind of false modesty. The reader who appreciates big band jazz, suddenly made uneasy by this kind of wording, might begin to wonder if "hybrid" signifies impurity more than cross-fertilization, if "popular" implies ephemeral more than widely appreciated. In fact, the second sentence states the same opinion as the first, the only addition being pomposity.

There are times when first person plural has a teaching or cooperative implication, and in these cases it ought to be kept and maintained. One might say, "we see, in example 2, a conscious use of archaic harmony," and it ought to be literally true: teacher (the author) and students (the readers) all see the harmony in question. "We now understand this to mean . . ." would simply be an extension of this idea; the teaching and explanation having taken place, author and readers now share an understanding and are on the same wavelength, thus "we." But the dividing line between "we understand" (following a clear explanation) and "we view" (which is perhaps just an ex cathedra statement of opinion or preference) can be very thin. In general, because of the negative effect first person plural can have on tone, it should be used with great care.

Passive Voice

Overuse of the passive voice is a common flaw in novice academic writing. Passive voice renders the object of an action, or the effect of a verb, into the subject of a sentence. That is: for the active construction "we made mistakes," where the subject of the sentence, *we*, is the agent or cause of the action, passive voice would have "mistakes were made." Notice that the original subject—the doer of the action—has completely disappeared. The action takes place in a shadow world where things happen without cause and responsibility for actions belongs elsewhere. Now compare the following passages:

Active voice

The development section makes extensive use of counterpoint, which propels the unstable harmony to several distant keys. This harmonic exploration reaches the dominant of the submediant (V/vi) at bar 70, and from that point a gradual

decrescendo and thinning of texture lead gently back to both
the tonic and recapitulation at bar 76.

Passive voice
    In the development, counterpoint is used extensively, and
the unstable harmony is propelled to several distant keys.
The dominant of the submediant (V/vi) is reached at bar 70,
and (after a gradual decrescendo and thinning of texture) the
tonic and recapitulation are reached at bar 76.

The second version is far less dynamic, and it implies that the musical events described occur in that bland universe where "mistakes were
made." The sheer sameness—"is used," "is propelled," "is reached," "are
reached"—tires the reader and implies that this laborious, blow-by-blow
description of musical events amounts to little of importance. The first
version, though, supplies an agent for every action, and a sense of continuity results. We see the passage in terms of compositional choices and
musical effects, which suggests a forward-moving musical narrative unfolding in real time.
    Passive voice is not necessarily wrong, however. Here is another
comparison.

It is disorienting, to say the least, when the recapitulation of
the main theme is presented in the subdominant rather than
the tonic.

It is disorienting, to say the least, when the composer presents the recapitulation of the main theme in the subdominant rather than the tonic.

In this case, the idea is better stated in passive than active voice. We *know*
that the composer is responsible for compositional choices in a work, and
the whole point is that a main theme returns in an unexpected key, not
that the composer flexed his muscles and took action and
composed. To say "the composer presents" in this context seems an
unwarranted intrusion: we were discussing musical events, not the composer's (here, obvious and unremarkable) invisible hand. But in this case
the passive voice is used but once; it does not appear often enough to

anaesthetize the reader, and there is no doubt about who is responsible for the event.

Traditional Academic Organization

Term papers, master's theses, doctoral dissertations, and scholarly articles often follow a particular plan of organization. With the laudable goal of clarity, this plan dictates that the writer begin a study with a brief statement of its contents, in the form of a fleshed-out outline, and that this same material also appear throughout the body of the paper, and then again in the conclusion. For example, an introduction might state:

> First, I will identify several examples of this type of monophonic writing in nineteenth- and twentieth-century American music. Next, it will be demonstrated that its origins lie in the work-chants of the colonial slaves in the New World. Finally, the significance of this music to both musicology and Colonial Studies in general will be evaluated.

This passage would benefit from less passive voice and substantial editing. For example: "Examples of this kind of monophony are found in nineteenth-century American music, and its origins lie in the work-chants of the colonial slaves, making the music significant both for musicology and Colonial Studies." But even if this passage were to remain three sentences in length, it might be the basis for a workable beginning, particularly if the uses of passive voice were amended. Still, it is really more outline than true prose paragraph; the sentences don't follow naturally, one from the other, but rather shadow a narrative that would take much longer than three sentences. When an outline serves as beginning, the temptation is for authors to keep touching base with it in the course of the paper. In such cases, the difference between informing the reader where in the process she or he is—a good idea—and merely reiterating the outline can be easily missed.

Consider the second sentence of this introduction: "Next, it will be demonstrated that its origins lie in the work-chants of the colonial slaves in the New World." In the body of the paper, this point might reappear in several ways. After the examples have been identified, as the section on origins is about to begin:

> We will see that the source musics of this American monophony are to be found in colonial work-chants.

After the origins, and immediately before the music's significance for musicology and Colonial Studies is discussed:

> As has been shown, the work-chants of the colonial slaves provided the source material for these surviving examples of American monophonic music.

Finally, as part of the conclusions:

> Colonial work-chants, as has been demonstrated, were the point of origin of this kind of uniquely American solo song.

Clearly, the author has not adequately developed the point (although it may be developed elsewhere), he or she is merely repeating it, to soporific effect. It is a good idea, whenever recapitulating a thought or touching base with the broader structure, to *make sure there is something new in the sentence,* either an elaboration of the idea or a clear transition to or from another point. The author reminds the reader where he or she is, while at the same time moving forward and doing something that was not previously done. Two examples:

> We will now see that the source musics of this American monophony are to be found in colonial work-chants, particularly the chants of the native workers most closely involved with the colonials' domestic lives.

> While we can see that colonial work-chants were in some sense the point of origin of this kind of uniquely American solo song, the transformation of this music was so radical that the practical idea of "origin" has to be reevaluated.

Continuity and momentum require that no sentence duplicate another, even for the good purpose of clarifying organization. Rather than clarify, a sentence that duplicates tends to show the seams in the outline with no compensating benefit. Particularly in a multisection academic paper, the author cannot afford to go over the same ground again and again.

Another common feature of academic writing is the so-called literature review. Required in many theses and dissertations, this is a section (often a separate chapter) devoted exclusively to earlier research related to one's topic of interest, with brief summaries and critiques of each item. While in some cases a review of the literature provides helpful background, more often it results in a turgid, mechanically written selection—often quite lengthy—that contributes little to the progress of the work. It is unnecessary, in most cases, to explain why previous scholarship has fallen short; better would be a separate annotated bibliography provided to the professor or academic committee, with earlier sources being cited in the body of the work only as relevant. Authors will ultimately be the best judges of when such treatments of previous literature should be included.

Even the best and most vibrant academic writing cannot exist without parenthetical elaborations and explanations, citations and critiques of earlier work, advanced vocabulary, and other easily satirized characteristics. The key lies in the restrained use of such things, so that their effectiveness is not diminished. As in musical analysis, the challenge is to find a judicious balance between subtlety and what is easily comprehended, remembering that both academic writing and the thought it communicates are challenging, and that readers must expect to rise to this challenge themselves.

FASHIONING CLEAR SENTENCES

"Less is more," a familiar saying, holds true in the formulation of sentences. While complex syntax can be a positive style trait, academic authors (student and professional alike) too often get lost in tangents and elaborations. Consider this sentence:

> The problems resulting from defining the formal content of Chopin's Ballades in terms of sonata form (or style, or process, or principle) only serve to complicate further the task of the critic, scholar, and performer, for while the Ballades share with sonata form certain analogous features (contrasting themes, contrasting key areas, development or expansion of thematic and motivic material), after thorough examination they may be seen to represent much less than the totality of the Ballade-narrative, and ultimately suggest that a wholly untraditional analytical approach is better suited to the task.

This 92-word sentence is not even particularly complex; it just appears that way because of all the asides. Too many words confuse rather than explain: the reader begins to lose sight of whether the subject of the sentence is the problems resulting from the original comparison, as first stated, or the Ballades themselves, or the analogous features in the two forms. Which of these necessitates a new approach? The primary culprit here is distance: so many words occur between "problems," "after thorough examination they," and "ultimately suggest" that the various stated plural items run together in the reader's mind: problems, Ballades, and analogous features.

Four principal ideas make up the sentence:

- the idea that there are problems resulting from a sonata-form approach to the Ballades, and that these problems complicate analysis
- what the similarities between the Ballades and sonata form are
- that these similarities do not account for enough of the works' content to support analysis in these terms
- the call for a new analytical approach

While it may not be necessary to devote a separate sentence to each idea, taken together they are far too much for one; two well-ordered, severely pruned sentences would be far preferable.

Trimming is the first priority. To speak of "defining the formal content . . . in terms of sonata form" is repetitious; how else to define formal content except in terms of form? Rather, we *view* or *analyze* works in the context of one or more particular forms. The first parenthesis is unnecessary; "sonata form" will do just fine, because this is not the place to debate whether "form" is the best way to describe one of the most commonly studied and identified compositional processes of the eighteenth and nineteenth centuries. The remaining parenthetical material, which explains the similarities between the Ballades and sonata form, needs to be brought closer to the first mention of the sonata idea and shortened.

We can recast the opening idea to explain the sonata-Ballade comparison with greater clarity. Since there will be a logical change of direction—that is, there are similarities but they will not prove definitive—let's begin with "although" ("while" would also work):

Although Chopin's Ballades have such typical sonata-form characteristics as contrasting themes and key areas and thematic development,

Rather than introducing other issues, it will be better to follow this single line of thought, namely where these similarities will or will not lead. To this end, we retrieve an idea from later in the original sentence and end up with sufficient material for a shorter, clearer statement:

> Although Chopin's Ballades have such typical sonata-form characteristics as contrasting themes and key areas and thematic development, these aspects represent much less than the totality of the Ballade-narrative.

The original sentence refers to the "task" of the critic, scholar, and performer. Which task is shared by these people? Rather than leave this vague task to the imagination of the reader, it would be better to save a few words and name it—say, analysis. The phrase "after thorough examination may be seen to represent" is unnecessary; we assume that the author has examined the works thoroughly, and we do not require reassurance. At the end, "wholly untraditional" may be replaced by "new," saving one word (but six syllables). The remaining ideas, that analysis is complicated rather than facilitated by sonata-Ballade linkage and that a new model is needed, make more sense combined than they do separated, as they are in the original version. An economical way of putting them might be:

> The sonata model thus causes more problems than it solves in the analysis of these pieces, and it seems clear that a new analytical approach is called for.

Together, these two sentences comprise 58 words, less than two-thirds the length of the original single sentence, and they present its ideas more clearly and elegantly. Elegance in writing—more a matter of simplicity and proportion than of linguistic curlicues—consists chiefly of a balance between three things: economy, the logical presentation of ideas, and an attractive variety in wording and syntax. But an overemphasis on economy results in curtness, an obsessive attention to logical presentation at the expense of other considerations can produce mechanical writing, and exaggerating an attractive variety makes for mannered and often florid prose. Striving to retain and balance these three qualities will eventually produce writing that is both clear and enjoyable to read.

Taste

Elegance is also a matter of taste, and it is the responsibility of every author to exercise restraint in the choice of language and metaphor, and wisdom in the consideration of what readers will appreciate, or *not* appreciate, seeing in print. Here is a passage by Cuthbert Girdlestone on the finale of Mozart's piano concerto in B-flat major, K. 456:

> The second subject then displays its lopsided mass; it advances with the nimble haste of a cripple, one of whose crutches has been stolen, and who pursues the thief brandishing the other. The woodwinds mock it and, when it changes places and gives itself to the oboe and bassoon, the piano jeers at it too.[4]

To quote Chaucer's Pardoner, "What needeth it to sermone of it more?" Although Girdlestone strives for the common touch by calling up an image all readers might be able to imagine, it tells us almost nothing about the music it purportedly describes. The image is so grotesquely pathetic, moreover, that it negates any imagined benefits of stylistic liveliness or unpretentiousness. This sort of lapse of taste, authors may safely assume, will *never* carry with it enough compensating merit to be worthwhile.

An aside here: the use of the word *cripple* reminds us that older sources frequently use terminology and reflect worldviews that cannot be presented today without qualification. The direct quotation or excerpting of such sources should not be restricted in an academic environment, but by the same token it should be done within the proper context, with explanation, judicious use of paraphrase, and so on. For example, racist passages by Richard Wagner or Daniel Gregory Mason (which I do *not* quote here) need not necessarily be quoted in all their ugly particulars, and when particulars are quoted, it is only appropriate to do so with contextual explanation and with a specific goal in mind.

Gender-Neutral Wording and the Pronoun Problem

A related issue is that of gender-neutral wording. English has a bit of a problem with the singular personal pronoun, which is either masculine or feminine but not undetermined: to refer to a person, we have *he* and *she* and that's all. Formerly, the masculine form was considered an inclusive singular form: "he" implied "he or she." In recent decades, however, we have become more aware of the subtle marginalizing or exclusionary effects, however unconscious, of such wordings. One solution sometimes

[4]Cuthbert Girdlestone, *Mozart and His Piano Concertos* [1948] (Norman, OK: University of Oklahoma Press, 1952), 274. Girdlestone is discussing the deployment of thematic material in the finale of Mozart's piano concerto K. 456 in B-flat.

seen is alternating uses of *he* and *she*; this rather contrived approach invites other complications such as creating the impression of irrational inconsistency or (depending on authorial bias) the possibility of using one pronoun positively and the other negatively. Currently, *he* and *she* are both restrictive, so unless one gender or the other is explicitly meant a different solution is necessary. It is true that "he or she" (or the reverse) is a bit awkward, but it can often serve—the compensating merit being the lack of exclusionary tone. In other cases, resourceful wording can obviate the need for a pronoun at all, or a general sentence can be reworded in the plural to avoid the problem. (Another example of a historically exclusionary usage that is now being treated differently is the year designations B.C. and A.D.—"Before Christ" and "Anno Domini" [in the year of Our Lord]. These are now seen as exclusively Christian in worldview, so the designations B.C.E. and C.E.—"Before the Common Era" and "Common Era"—are used instead.)

A lazy solution for the he-and-she problem that is heard often in spoken English (and often seen in writing, particularly in British sources) is the use of "they," which is *only* a plural form, instead of "he or she." The ugliness of this solution is seen in a phrase like "when a person picks up the violin, they need to . . ." More complex is this statement about the famous tubist and pedagogue Arnold Jacobs: "One common technique Jacobs used with beginning students was to take their horn from them and play a few simple notes on it." Yes, we know what the author means, and but it is still an ugly construction and must be avoided. Better is the following: "One of Jacobs's favorite techniques was to take a beginning student's horn and play a few simple notes," because "student" and "horn" are both singular. Usually a little careful rewording fixes the problem: "When violinists prepare to play, they need to . . . " The best general rule is a favorite of piano teachers (sometimes attributed to Chopin): "Look closely at every difficulty. You will uncover a jewel." It is as true in writing as it is in piano playing. The best solution is often to devote the modicum of additional time to rewriting the sentence, so as to craft something clearer and more creative that avoids the problem entirely.

Transitions

Transitions are words and phrases that lead from one idea to another, relating the new idea to the idea preceding it in a particular way, guiding the reader through the author's line of thought. Examples of such relationships include *amplification* (for which one might use "furthermore," "moreover," or "in addition"), *contrast* or *qualification* ("but," "however," "on the other hand"), and *illustration* ("for example," "for instance," "take as an example"). Perhaps the second idea intensifies the first, perhaps it is a logical result of the first, perhaps it contrasts or contradicts the previous idea or stands apart from it in some way; the relationship of the two ideas will tell you which transitional word or phrase to use. "Moreover," for example, indicates that the writer will develop the point further. "On the other hand" indicates that the writer will go on to make a point somewhat contrary to what has just been said. These kinds of transitions, including "incidentally," "nonetheless," and "in conclusion," often make the difference between a passage that is clear and easy to follow and what seems to be a random succession of sentences.

Imagine a discussion of slow introductions to sonata-allegro movements that covers both early uses of this device and a later, more famous piece that many now assume to have been the first use in a sonata for solo piano. In the course of such a discussion, one might see this paragraph:

> Beethoven's use of the slow introduction is a case in point. The first movement of his op. 13 piano sonata ("Pathétique") is often considered revolutionary in its use of this device, usually seen to this point only in the opening movements of symphonies. The material from this introduction reappears two more times in the course of the movement, not just at the beginning. The Italian composer Muzio Clementi used a slow introduction in his piano sonata op. 34/2, composed two to three years before the "Pathétique." Clementi's introductory material provides the basis of the rest of the movement, which was not true of Beethoven's, and this material returns in more varied guises. Beethoven's movement is neither the first, nor the most adventurous, early use of the slow introduction in a piano sonata.

This paragraph makes a kind of sense, but the continuity is rather awkward. There are too many jumps between ideas and little flow. Here is the same paragraph, with transitions added in brackets:

> Beethoven's use of the slow introduction is a case in point. The first movement of his op. 13 piano sonata ("Pathétique") is often considered revolutionary in its use of this device, usually seen to this point only in the opening movements of symphonies. [Moreover,] The material from this introduction

reappears two more times in the course of the movement, not just at the beginning. [But] The Italian composer Muzio Clementi used a slow introduction in his piano sonata op. 34/2, composed two to three years before the "Pathétique." [Significantly,] Clementi's introductory material provides the basis of the rest of the movement, which was not true of Beethoven's, and this material returns in more varied guises. [Therefore, despite its reputation] Beethoven's movement is neither the first, nor the most adventurous, early use of the slow introduction in a piano sonata.

Transitions signal when an idea contrasts with what preceded it, when it turns a corner, or follows logically, or intensifies the previous idea. On a general level, they ensure a continuity of thought that would not have been apparent from the mere succession of ideas.

Variety

Variety is an aspect of writing in which a musical comparison is particularly valuable. If we imagine a piece of music with equal (say, four-bar) phrasing throughout, with no variation in textural or harmonic complexity or lyrical interest, we envision boredom. Consider a prose equivalent:

Music of the American Indians is of increasing interest today. Serious study of Native American musics is a relatively recent phenomenon. Some nineteenth-century composers sought to incorporate Indian elements in their compositions. The twentieth century saw a fully developed school of Indianist composition. The resulting works were *about* Indians rather than being in any way musically authentic. Most American listeners remained largely ignorant of true Native American music. Current research seeks to fill this gap in American musical understanding.

The succession of similarly constructed sentences numbs by its very sameness. Consider, instead:

Music of the American Indians is of increasing interest today. Serious study of actual Native American musics is, however, a relatively recent phenomenon. Although some nineteenth-century composers sought, tentatively, to incorporate Indian elements in their compositions, it wasn't until the twentieth century that a fully developed school of Indianist composition evolved. The resulting works were *about* Indians rather than being in any way musically authentic. As a result, most American listeners remained largely ignorant of true Native American music. One of the central goals of current research, then, is filling this gap in American musical understanding.

The passage is greatly improved in both rhythm and continuity simply by combining some sentences and adding transitions and other continuity cues. These cues include "however," which suggests a conditional relationship to the previous idea; "although," which implies that the following idea is about to be contradicted or superseded, and is offered for that purpose; and "then" (in the final sentence), which signals a dependence or logical-effect relationship with what came before—all of which alert the reader to the train of thought laid out by the author. The passage is easier to follow, and the variety in sentence structure and length refreshes the mind of the reader rather than (as might first be expected) presenting an additional challenge. In general, variety is the spice of lively writing: a lengthy sentence is often best followed by a simple and direct one, and next may come one with parallel construction, and all of them may be contrasted by a sentence with a parenthetical explanation or aside. The key is to follow no rule, but rather to avail oneself of all the variety the English language affords.

PUNCTUATION

The purpose of punctuation, in English or any other language, is to divide and separate thoughts so that they are most easily understood. Sometimes differences in punctuation result in differences in meaning:

> Musicians who are underpaid should strike.

> Musicians, who are underpaid, should strike.

The first sentence, which has no punctuation other than the final period, states that those musicians who are underpaid should strike. The second, which puts "who are underpaid" as a parenthetical phrase between two commas, says instead that *all* musicians are underpaid and that they all should strike. The first sentence identifies "musicians who are underpaid" as a subset of all musicians, and it is this group of musicians that is the subject of the sentence, while the second sentence uses "who are underpaid" as a parenthetical descriptor of *all* musicians, leaving "musicians" alone as the subject. The difference in meaning between the two sentences is substantial.

More often, though, punctuation does not change meaning this radically. It governs rhythm and flow—what is sometimes considered the musical aspect of writing. Ideas are separated from each other by periods, commas, semicolons, colons, and dashes for clarification, much as we clarify our meaning when we speak with pauses of different lengths for breathing and dramatic effect. One good way to check punctuation is to read drafts of your writing aloud; if you misread a passage, the chances are good that the punctuation is at fault.

Colon, Semicolon, and Comma

The colon, semicolon, and comma are frequently confused, but each has specific uses. The *colon* temporarily stops a sentence and announces to the reader that a quotation, a list of items, an explanation, or an example will follow. (It is also used in numerical ratios and times of day.)

> The essential dances of the Baroque suite are these: Allemande, Courante, Sarabande, and Gigue.

The *semicolon* is a fairly lengthy pause that separates independent clauses (that is, clauses that can stand as complete sentences), as in this example:

> Brahms had no need of learning the Hungarian-Gypsy style from Reményi; it had been popular for decades before their first meeting.

Semicolons also separate elements in a list, either when the list is inordinately long or when certain of the elements require shorter pauses for additional information. Here is an expanded version of the first example:

> Traditional dances of the Baroque suite are these: Allemande; Courante, or occasionally Corrente; Sarabande; Gigue, or occasionally Giga; and such optional movements as Gavotte, Bourée, or Air.

The *comma*, finally, is the punctuation mark that signifies the shortest pause, merely a figurative intake of breath. A pair of commas is often used to enclose a parenthetical or explanatory clause (as in the second of the two sentences about underpaid musicians, above), and it is the commonest of errors to omit one comma or the other. In this context, they are best thought of as parentheses:

> Eric Clapton's recordings, his blues background notwithstanding, embrace a wide variety of styles.

The dash (sometimes called the em dash, after the printer's measurement of its length, which is the width of an M) provides an interruptive pause and is often used for authorial asides—asides that step a bit farther out than parentheses or parenthetical commas. Sometimes it is written with two hyphens, such as on certain electronic mail (email) programs that don't have a full character set, but word-processing programs all have the actual dash, which should be used. Both the dash and the substitute hyphens are used without spaces before or after.

> In Bartók's music, time signatures that seem to be metrical anomalies—at least within the traditional Western repertoire—are in fact rooted in ancient Hungarian folk music.

> Interpretations of bel canto opera are too often marred by fidelity to the score—fidelity that would have been unthinkable by the opera singers of the bel canto eras, who gained fame through the virtuosity of their ornamentation.

But be careful not to use too many dashes. An abundance of dashes can give your writing the sense of being punchy and overly emphatic, or (conversely) it can give the impression of directionlessness, suggesting that you cannot write without interrupting yourself. This is a danger in academic writing, where authors often unconsciously sacrifice focus and momentum because they want so much to squeeze in every last bit of even marginally relevant information and accommodate every possible interpretation or implication. Summary: *Keep your eye on the ball!*

A Note on Hyphens and Centuries

This is not the place for an exhaustive treatment of the hyphen, but one common error needs mention: novice writers often forget that century designations follow the pattern of adjectival compounds. When an adjective describes a noun, there is no hyphen: *music of the thirteenth century.* When both the adjective and the noun are used to describe another noun, they are combined with a hyphen: *thirteenth-century music.*

Specifically Musical Uses of Punctuation

Certain conventions of punctuation are used in connection with generic titles of classical works, particularly where performance indications serve as section titles. The movement is usually separated from the performance or mood indication by a colon (Minuet: Andante). Performance indications are separated from each other by a semicolon (thus the first movement of a Haydn symphony might be designated Largo; Allegro), and movements are separated from each other, when they are not given separate lines in the program, by em dashes: Allegro—Adagio—Allegro.

With respect to titles in general, we distinguish between titles of complete works and sections within them through formatting and punctuation—italics (or, as a weak second choice for people writing long-hand or using old typewriters, underlining, which should *never* be substituted for italics when word processing) for complete works, and quotation marks for parts thereof. Thus, one of the songs in Robert Schumann's song cycle *Dichterliebe* is "Aus alten Märchen." Even though it is customary to italicize foreign words, when an entire foreign phrase appears within quotation marks it is generally not done because it looks too fussy.

ACCURACY IN WORDING

Nothing can call an author's competence into question like the choice of the wrong word, such as when *mitigate* (to moderate, or make less severe) and *militate* (to have force or influence) are confused; one can militate against something, but one cannot mitigate against anything, despite how often that construction is seen. Similar pitfalls are presented by the pairs *comprise* and *compose, imply* and *infer,* and *complimentary* and *complementary,* which sound similar (or identical) but mean different things. For the first pair, the rule is best memorized: *the whole comprises the parts, and the parts compose the whole.* Thus, a Baroque dance suite comprises at least four different dance movements, but an Allemande, Courante, Sarabande, and Gigue compose (or make up, or constitute) the Baroque dance suite. With *imply* and *infer,* both words pertain to what is hinted or guessed at; the distinction has to do with who is responsible for the conclusions. *Imply* has to do with meaning or significance suggested by words or actions (that is, latent within the subject itself), whereas *infer* reflects assumptions made or conclusions drawn (i.e., made by someone outside the subject in question):

> Milhaud's use of jazz in *Le Création du monde* implies his awareness of its growing popularity.

> We can infer, from Milhaud's use of jazz in *Le Création du monde,* that he was aware of its growing popularity.

Complimentary and *complementary* seem to be especially confusing. One pays a compliment, and one receives a free ticket "with the compliments of the management," thus it is a "complimentary ticket," or "comp." A complement is something that completes something else, making it greater or better. Thus, "Complementary areas of expertise for music scholars might differ according to specialty, with history or language study being helpful for musicologists, anthropology being appropriate for ethnomusicologists, and mathematics or computer science being ideal for music theorists."

A comprehensive list of similar word-pairs and problematic terms would be impossibly long. But authors must repeatedly be urged that *accuracy in wording is crucial.* Make sure that you are aware of both specific meaning (*denotation*), and the implication (*connotation*) of the words you use. To say

> The work was in a $\frac{3}{4}$ rhythm, and had the character of a waltz

is to commit an error of denotation, because $\frac{3}{4}$ time is a meter, not a rhythm. Rhythm and meter have very different meanings (see below), although "rhythm" is often wrongly used for both. Saying

> The composer drags the tempo in this phrase

when what is intended is

> The composer directs that this phrase be played *ritardando*

is an error of connotation, because "drags" is a negative word, suggesting sluggishness and heaviness, while *ritardando* explains that the tempo simply slows down.

Ill-Advised Upgrades

A subcategory of problematic word choices is what might be called *upgrades,* where an author seeks to "improve" a word, to give it additional weight or importance, by using a more pretentious version of it. Sometimes this can simply be funny, as when an archaic word like "whilst" is given the job for which "while" is ready and waiting. More damaging is when the author is unaware of a difference of meaning, as when "simple" becomes "simplistic" (oversimplified), amuse becomes "bemuse" (to be puzzled or confused), or—best of all—when "ultimate" becomes "penultimate." The author is thinking "I mean *really* the ultimate," whereas penultimate actually means the next to last. (For the record, "antepenultimate" means the one before the next to last.)

Wording that is only superficially accurate is also best changed, such as in the sentence "In the closing section, the composer repeats the primary theme verbatim." It is true that one of the meanings of "verbatim" is "exactly," but the literal meaning comes from Latin, "word for word." To repeat a theme, or any group of musical notes, word for word is impossible. The error here is only partially one of denotation, since one of the meanings of the word is acceptable; rather, the word *verbatim* is simply an inelegant choice, much better corrected than allowed to stand.

Beat, Meter, Rhythm

The words *beat, meter,* and *rhythm*, all of which have to do with the measurement of musical time, are probably the most often confused words in the musical lexicon. *Beat* is simply a pulse, that which marks time in regular intervals. *Meter* is the regular organizing of beats, for example in repeating groups of three or four, and assigning at least one beat in each group (often the first) greater importance or emphasis. *Rhythm* is any sequence of durations, repeated or not. Dances, historically, have had characteristic rhythms associated with them, such as dotted eighth note-sixteenth note-eighth note in a $\frac{6}{8}$ or $\frac{12}{8}$ meter for the siciliano:

or a dotted-quarter-eighth-quarter-quarter in a slow $\frac{4}{4}$ for a pavane:

That and Which

In American (as opposed to British) English there is a clear distinction between *that* and *which*. (This despite the common, somewhat lazy practice of using *which* in virtually all cases, which adds a slightly fussy and pretentious tone, at least to American ears.) *That* is a restrictive pronoun; it distinguishes the item under discussion from like items. For example, "the cello that soars out over the rest of the ensemble" suggests one cello among several, or many, acting in a specific way. By contrast, *which* is nonrestrictive; it indicates that there is no further limitation on the indicated object. "The cello, which soars out over the rest of the ensemble" indicates that there is only one cello in the ensemble, and (for the moment at least) it enjoys a solo role. In cases of uncertainty, one convenient (if not *always* correct) method is to look for a parenthetical phrase within commas; *which* usually follows a comma, while *that* rarely does.

Accuracy in Spelling and Punctuation

There is nothing more to be said here about spelling and punctuation other than *do it right!* Your computer's spell-checking software will not catch every error, particularly when homophones (e.g., *led* and *lead, past* and *passed, to* and *too*) are involved. Similarly, the fact that much of the English-speaking world seems unaware of the difference between "it's" (the contraction of *it is*) and "its" (the possessive; something belonging to *it*) does not mean that such carelessness is somehow excusable in writing. (Note: *never* write a word spelled i-t-s-apostrophe. It doesn't exist.) Likewise, there is no excuse for inserting an apostrophe before an "s" that creates a plural. Errors of this kind bespeak not only ignorance but slovenliness; it is as if the author is either unable or lazily disinclined to spell or punctuate accurately. In either case, it is a message no author can afford to send.

Aggregate Titles

Musical works frequently have plural titles, such as *Piano Variations.* Such works are considered as wholes and therefore are singular. For example, it is correct to say "Brahms's *Variations on a Theme of Händel* has always been popular among pianists" (not "*have* always been popular") because this is a single work, even though it comprises many different variations. By comparison, there would be no problem with saying

"Brahms's variations *have* always been popular among pianists," because he wrote not only many variations but also several variation sets, and no specific set is designated here; the subject is unquestionably plural.

Awkward Wording

The final arbiter of good writing is not a stylebook or some other external authority, but rather—as suggested before—the reader's ear. Phrases that make the reader stumble, hesitate, or reread them must be changed, whether or not they are grammatically correct. As a general rule, a phrase or sentence that troubles you for any reason should be taken back to the workshop; a much better solution undoubtedly awaits.

Obvious infelicities include constructions such as "one such example appears in Example 3" or "the same figure appears in Figure 4." There is nothing actually wrong with what is being said, but the repetition of "example" and "figure" when the second uses have different meanings confounds the reader. Any coincidental repetition of a word, as opposed to repetition for rhetorical emphasis or clarity, merits close scrutiny and (likely) adjustment.

Try to detect awkwardness of any kind—wording, poor treatment of transitions, ambiguity of meaning—in the proofreading process. As these are subtler matters than spelling, punctuation, and subject-verb agreement, practice and experience will be the best guides in learning what to look for and how to rectify problematic passages. Cultivating a dependable "writer's ear," an instinctive sense of the rhythm and flow of the language, is a long-term (indeed, an unending) process. All authors, in addition to perfecting their own writing, must therefore read a great deal, assimilating as much as possible from the writing they find most effective.

TOWARD A PERSONAL STYLE

There is no more valuable advice on the subject of writing style than that of E. B. White: "To achieve style, begin by affecting none—that is, place yourself in the background."[5] The priority is your subject; strive for clear

---

[5]William Strunk, Jr., and E. B. White, *The Elements of Style*, 4th ed. (New York: Longman, 2000), 70.

communication, not to make an impression. Similar advice has long been given to nervous musical performers: worry about the *music,* not how well you're doing. Letting go of the ego in such a situation will, paradoxically, produce writing far more likely to reflect well upon its author (and performances of which the interpreter can be proud).

White also gave the payoff for this advice, in a timeless phrase: "No writer long remains incognito."[6] From diligent, intelligent work on writing, a unique voice inevitably results.

[6]Ibid., 67.

9

THE FINAL MANUSCRIPT

Do the little things well; then will come the great things begging to be done.

—CHINESE PROVERB

GENERAL FORMAT

The following suggestions are intended to produce a paper that is easy to look at, read, and preserve. "Standard form," which all compilations of style guidelines purport to follow, is in fact not nearly so standard as it would be convenient to believe. The requirements of your editor or instructor, should they differ from the advice and examples given here, take precedence.

1. Binding, Paper, Duplication. Papers must be stapled, paper-clipped, bound in some way, or kept in an envelope (this last is most appropriate when submitting an article for publication). If your paper is a class assignment, ask if your instructor has a preference; do not overlook this matter and expect him or her to keep track of a pile of loose pages. Likewise, do not use any last-minute strategies like a crumpled upper-left-hand corner or a bobby pin. Make life easier for your reader, not harder! Pages are to be printed on one side only, and paper quality is to be good—not necessarily premium stationery, but not onionskin or newsprint either.

2. Word Processing. Use a computer with flexible and adaptable word-processing software such as Microsoft Word, WordPerfect, or any other you choose (my intent is to illustrate, not to advertise), and make sure this software has a footnote function—cut-and-paste editing of academic work without such a function is nearly impossible. If you are a student who does not own a computer with such software, the computer lab at your college or university will certainly have it, and you will discover that word-processing has countless other benefits. (Depending on another's computer carries a wider variety of risks than using your own, and you should back up your work more frequently, and store it in more than one place.) Some people no longer even accept papers that are handwritten or produced on a typewriter; handwriting should only be a last resort when specific health or coordination issues prevent the use of a keyboard. If you have not yet learned to use a traditional keyboard (the so-called qwerty keyboard, after the characters on the upper row of the left hand), and there is no physical reason why you cannot, learn now.

If you are not a student, and you do not have immediate access to a computer lab, simply remember that word-processed writing is standard in publishing—in fact, formal submission in both electronic form and in hard copy is usually required—and that the initial impression your paper or article makes will affect how well it is read and received. Many copy shops sell computer time, so even if you don't yet own a personal computer you can still write with one.

3. Copies. Always keep a photocopy or a second printed copy of your paper for yourself. Occasionally papers are lost, by student or professor, and a copy is the best safeguard against lost work. Of course you will keep your computer disks or CDs or USB flash drive or other external storage device with your manuscript, but these media are easily lost or damaged, and disks sometimes decay to the point of unreadability. If you are asked for a duplicate copy, replying that "I didn't bother to copy it and my computer crashed and I seem to have lost my school stuff when I changed apartments and anyway the different generations of the software cause translation problems" is not going to get you very far. A complete loss of work is a disaster—*your* disaster—and it is easily avoided.

Corollary: Save All Notes and Drafts. Keep all notes and drafts so that you can easily verify a quotation, a wording, a citation; your instructor or another scholar may need more background information than appears in the final draft. Also save your notes on computer, and save the files in more than one place. All your research (not just the final paper draft) constitutes a database, whether it consists of notes scrawled on notebook paper or a formal annotated bibliography, and you never know when in life you will want to return to it; it may be during the grading process or twenty years later.

4. Title Page and Pagination. Every paper should have a title page with the following information: title of the paper, name of assignment if appropriate (e.g., "Opinion Paper"), course number and name of course, professor's name, and date. When submitting an article for publication, the title page should have the title of the paper, the author's name, and the author's university or professional affiliation or city of residence. Often, to facilitate a blind review process, a journal or magazine will specify that article submissions should be anonymous, with the author identified only in the cover letter. In such cases, it is the author's responsibility to remove all information pertaining to his or her identity not only from the title page and running heads of the manuscript, but also from the text and footnotes. In an article or paper, pagination begins after the title page; in a book or book manuscript, pagination of the front matter (title page, publishing information, preface, and so on) is done in lower case roman numerals, and begins with the first page on which printing appears. Pagination of the text itself begins with arabic numeral 1.

5. Spacing and Margins. Double-space your paper, and use margins of between 1 and 1.5 inches. Where specific guidelines (such as university thesis formats that accommodate binding) contradict this, follow the specific guidelines. Pages with headings, such as the first pages of chapters, will need more space at the top. This arrangement of margins and spacing will provide relatively light text density, so the paper will be easy to read, with ample room for the instructor or editor to write comments.

6. Block Quotations. A block quotation does not use quotation marks unless someone is being quoted within it, in which case the quotation marks are used normally. Formatting it differently from the rest of the surrounding text obviates the need for quotation marks, which usually serve that function. Set off a quotation of more than two lines with an extra return before and after it, and by indenting an extra half-inch at both the left and right margins for the paragraph(s) of the quotation. The margins will now be wider than those of the rest of the paper, and the quotation will stand out from the text as a small "block." You do not need to change font or font size, though publishers often will. Block quotations are generally single spaced, except when journals specify that *everything* should be double-spaced in manuscript submissions. Because you will cite the quotation in a footnote or endnote, there will be a small superscript number at the end of the quotation. Put citation numbers outside—that is, after—every punctuation mark except the dash. (There are many examples of block quotations throughout this book. Citations will be discussed more fully below.)

7. Bibliography. Bibliographies are standard in books, are often provided for scholarly articles, but are never used for concert reviews, program notes, and other less formal kinds of writing. For classroom assignments, however, they are often required and are helpful for student and instructor alike. Since all the sources consulted in the course of research will probably not be found in the footnotes, a bibliography enables the author to report the full list, excluding informal sources like personal telephone conversations, personal interviews, and electronic mail (which will appear in the notes). For differences in punctuation, presentation, and content between notes and bibliographic entries, see the section Sample Citations.

ABBREVIATIONS

Latin Abbreviations and Terminology

Certain abbreviations and terminology found in academic writing serve to remind us of a bygone era when familiarity with the Latin language was the *sine qua non* of every educated individual. Although these conventions are becoming less frequent, they are found in enough sources that one needs to be familiar with them. Except for ibid., op. cit., and loc. cit., these may be used in the text as well as in footnotes.

cf.	*confer,* "compare"
e.g.	*exempli gratia,* "for example"
et al.	*et alia,* "and all," often used to indicate multiple authors
ibid.	*ibidem,* "as above," used for consecutive footnotes from a single source
i.e.	*id est,* "that is" (i.e. and e.g. are often confused, though they are not the same)
inf.	*infra,* "below," as in "for more on this subject, see *inf.*"
loc. cit.	*loco citato,* "in the place cited," an archaic form of indicating a previously cited article
olim	"once," meaning formerly

op. cit.   *opere citato,* "in the work cited," an archaic form of
                  indicating a previously cited book

passim   from *passus,* "scattered," indicating that a word or
                  idea occurs frequently throughout a work or passage

s.v.   *sub verbo,* "under the word," used to refer to
                  dictionary entries

Musical Abbreviations

There are certain abbreviations peculiar to writing about music that are commonly used. These include:

op.; opp.   opus; opera (*opera* meaning more than one work,
                  not, in this case, a musical-theatrical work such as
                  Puccini's *Turandot*)

m.; mm.   measure; measures (used only when designating by
                  measure number)

b.; bb.   bar; bars (more informal than m. and mm. and not
                  often used—and never, to my knowledge, in North
                  America)

p.; pp.   page; pages

MM or M.M.   metronome mark, as in (MM ♩ = 96); this
                  abbreviation is common, but there is probably no
                  real reason to maintain it when, in a discussion of
                  tempo, the simple (♩ = 96, or quarter note = 96) is
                  just as clear

Note: The word *bar* is acceptable only in nonspecific usage (e.g., "The recapitulation is reached some fifty bars later") and depending on the prevailing tone of the passage. It is becoming more common to say "at bar 5," but the abbreviations b. and bb. are only occasionally seen.

TITLES OF MUSICAL WORKS

Designations of musical works often provide title, key, performing forces, and opus or catalogue number. As with other typographical matters, it would be helpful if there were more agreement than there is. Here are some conventions designed to provide the necessary information as conveniently as possible.

Titles can be "true titles," such as *Don Giovanni* or *The Yellow River Concerto,* or generic titles like Mass or Sonata. True titles need to be in italics, and often the other information is omitted—one might not see Beethoven's biggest choral and orchestral work, *Missa Solemnis,* designated *Missa Solemnis,* op. 123 unless it is on a program listing. Generic titles (titles using the musical genre of the piece) are capitalized but not italicized, treated with somewhat less formality, and usually given key designations and perhaps catalogue numbers: Liszt's Sonata in B Minor, Brahms's Second Symphony, Beethoven's Sonata in E Minor, op. 90. Sonatas for piano alone often do not bear the additional "for Piano" in their titles, but sonatas for other instruments, and other instruments with piano, usually do. Leonard Bernstein's *Mass,* which uses a generic title as a true title, serves to illustrate the impossibility of perfect solutions.

"Opus 24" simply means that a particular piece is the twenty-fourth work the composer chose to publish, to present to the world. Conclusions about when a piece was composed cannot necessarily be drawn from publishing information of that kind, especially because publishers have added works to composers' catalogues after the composers were deceased. Other composers' works were catalogued long after by scholars whose names are used to designate the catalogue: Otto Erich Deutsch for Schubert (e.g., Quintet in C Major for Strings, D. 956), Ludwig Köchel for Mozart (e.g., Piano Concerto in A Major, K. 488), and so on. When there is a well-known popular name for a work, it should be included in parentheses this way: Chopin's Prelude in D-flat Major, op. 24, no. 15 ("Raindrop"). (When, as in the case of Chopin's Preludes, a single opus comprises more than one actual work, individual pieces are often designated, e.g., op. 24/15.) When a popular name for a work is not well known, such as "The Burning of Moscow" for the famous Prelude in C-Sharp Minor, op. 3/2 of Sergei Rachmaninov, *don't use it at all!* The majority of popular names originated not with the composers but with publishers, usually as marketing devices, and there is no reason to make them part of the title if they are not already firmly in public awareness.

In concert and recital programs, works must be given their full formal titles, including key and opus or catalogue number.

MUSICAL EXAMPLES AND CAPTIONS

Allow a quarter-inch between the top of a musical example and the text it follows, between the bottom of the example's caption and the text it precedes, and between the example itself and its caption. Place the caption beneath the example.

Production of Examples

For most classroom assignments, photocopied score examples, either collected at the end of a paper or pasted individually in between paragraphs of text, will be sufficient. (Your instructor may have different requirements, of course.) For graduate documents or works submitted for publication, it is far better to generate the examples you need with music-processing software such as *Finale* or *Sibelius,* or to pay someone to generate them. Such software enables authors to customize excerpts without having to include extra measures and to produce reductions that will be easier to read than full scores. (For works intended for publication, the musical examples need to be on separate sheets, not incorporated in the text.)

Works intended for publication and graduate documents to be bound and archived will require permissions for the use of copyrighted musical material. The legalities regarding fair use (that is, scholarly, non-profit use) of copyrighted material are complex, and it is necessary for authors to research each individual case, establish who holds the rights, and, when necessary, formally request permission for use. Obtaining permission will usually involve crediting the copyright holder in some way, usually on the page the example appears, and often it will require a fee. Music over seventy-five years old is generally within the public domain (meaning no longer under copyright), but a particular published *image* of it may not be; music-processing software will help in this situation. The rights to more recent music are often held by the publisher, and so—regardless of whether the examples are computer-generated or not—permissions must be obtained.

There are times, however, when it is better to leave examples out. When only passing reference is made to a musical passage, in a parenthetical context ("instances of the same phenomenon are found at the opening of Beethoven's *Der Glorreiche Augenblick* and in measures 4–5 of Stephen Foster's 'Camptown Races,' but these were written later than the Paradis example under discussion"), the reader can often do without the musical examples; the passages in question can be located for verification, if need be. A score example may also be avoided for reasons of familiarity; most readers will not need to review, say, the opening four notes of Beethoven's Fifth Symphony. Nor is it likely that many readers will need to see familiar popular songs (such as those by the Beatles) in notated form, though exceptional cases might involve the discussion of a specific melodic inflection or instrumental solo. In general, economy and restraint are as relevant to score examples as they are to words, and authors need to weigh the inclusion of each musical excerpt.

Captions

Every score example requires an individual caption, designated "Ex." for "example" (not "Fig." for "figure," which designates a chart, graph, or other illustration). Examples need to be numbered individually (i.e., Ex. 1, Ex. 2, etc.), and they may be put in subgroups (Ex. 1a, Ex. 1b, etc.) when the context demands it, as for instance a cluster of short, musically related motives, or different snippets of the same section of a piece. In multi-chapter works such as theses, dissertations, and books, it is best to number them according to chapter: those of chapter one will be numbered Ex. 1.1, 1.2, and 1.3; those of chapter two Ex. 2.1, 2.2, and so on.

Two basic schools of thought govern the contents of captions. One holds that each caption ought to have only the minimum necessary material: composer, piece, movement if necessary, and measure numbers of the passage provided. For large scores with rehearsal numbers or letters but no numbered measures, it is common to use an indication such as "R2+3"—designating three measures after the measure marked with rehearsal number 2. The first time a work is excerpted in a musical example, the caption needs to consist of the following:

Ex. 1.1. [Firstnameoptional] Composerlastname, *Full Formal Title of Work,* mm. xxx–xx. [Remember, generic titles are not italicized.]

All subsequent references to the same work may take an abbreviated form:

Ex. 1.2. Lastname, *Short Title,* mm. xx–xxx.

For this approach, the only function of the caption is to identify the score example, with any additional information about it appearing in the text and footnotes. One advantage is the ease of formatting; such captions can often be kept to one line, so typesetting and layout are relatively uncomplicated.

The other school of thought regards each musical example as operating both in relation to the main text and independently of it. A caption might therefore give far more information about the musical excerpt shown, such as its publisher, what the reader should be looking for in the excerpt, and other particulars. Such a caption might read:

> Ex. 38. Rossini, *Il barbiere di Siviglia,* "Una voce poco fa," mm. 41–42, version of Cinti-Damoreau. To judge by the number of ornamented versions that survive in the notebooks of famous opera singers of the time, Rossini's published version provided only a suggestion of what a singer would actually perform.

The benefits to this approach include:

- Additional material pertinent to the excerpted score itself is presented in close proximity to it.
- The continuity of the text is not cluttered with tangential material.
- Certain kinds of information are thereby much easier for the reader to go back and find if needed.

On the minus side:

- Typesetting and formatting are much more problematic.
- There is the possibility of the discussion becoming fragmented, with key elements remaining in the caption rather than in the text proper.

Ultimately, this is a matter of taste, to be decided by the individual author, course instructor, or publisher, depending on the situation. Even when the content-intensive approach to captions is used, it is best for all salient points to appear in the text proper, so as to avoid a diffuse argument.

THE CITATION PROCESS

Citations have two primary functions. First, they tell the reader—should the reader want to know, and reading the citations ought always to be the reader's option—where to find information that the author drew upon. Such information, whether in the form of direct quotations or paraphrases, must be cited properly, and these citations give appropriate credit for thoughts not the author's own. Second, proper citations allow readers to access the same sources the author did, to follow the author's train of thought, to proceed in different directions from these sources, and ultimately to evaluate the author's use and understanding of them. More information about when to cite sources is to be found in Chapter 6.

Citation formats vary somewhat throughout the English-speaking world. For the United States, a concise and convenient source is D. Kern Holoman, *Writing About Music* (Berkeley and Los Angeles: University of California Press, 1988).[1] This work, a style manual for the prominent musicology journal *Nineteenth-Century Music,* also provides guidance on a wide variety of other matters such as terminology, capitalization schemes, syllabification, and musical example formats. A standard source, particularly regarding academic documents and details of citation form, is Kate L. Turabian, *A Manual for Writers of Term Papers, Theses, and Dissertations,* 6th ed. (Chicago and London: University of Chicago Press, 1996), which is a user-friendly summary of the standard academic format authority, the *Chicago Manual of Style.* Note, however, that Turabian's *Manual* offers advice for a variety of disciplines and formats, so it must be used carefully, with the specific requirements of your situation in mind.

Footnotes or Endnotes?

There is no difference in format between footnotes and endnotes; they read precisely the same way, and the sample footnote citations below can also be used for endnotes. Word-processing programs will produce either, and switch between them, and some are able to maintain both systems simultaneously. As to which is preferable: George Bernard Shaw once complained that reading a footnote was like having to go downstairs and answer the door when one was making love. Others find footnotes less offensive, and prefer to have the choice of whether or not to look down to the foot of the page—that action, like answering the door, being a matter of choice. With footnotes, at least the reader needn't flip to the end of the paper, book, or (worst) chapter to pursue the note. Neither way is more correct than the other, so the decision belongs to the author, instructor, and/or editor and publisher.

---

[1] I differ with Holoman on a small number of points. One of these is his preference for leaving the name of the publisher out of footnote citations; I agree with the many who include it. He indicates page numbers with p. or pp.; I think these indications are unnecessary, and that the numbers themselves at the ends of footnotes are self-explanatory. Again: these are differences of opinion on specific points; you will find that there are minute differences among *all* style guides and that there is really no such thing as standard form.

Parenthetical Citation Format

Turabian provides instructions for another commonly used citation system: parenthetical author-date format. Certain musical disciplines, such as Music Education and Ethnomusicology, follow this practice, though there are some differences between the Chicago Manual and American Psychological Association (APA) systems. (Music Theory seems to use both.) The Turabian/Chicago Manual version is illustrated in the following example:

> The value of the sonata form designation is that it "presumes a dialectical presentation of ideas" (Fieldman 2002, 145).

Substituting a colon for the comma and space is also acceptable, thus: (Fieldman 2002:145). APA format, generally favored by the Music Education discipline, would have a comma in between the author and date. Parenthetical author-date citation systems depend upon the bibliography, sometimes called a reference list, to which the reader then turns. The date identifies which work by this author is meant when more than one work by the same author is listed. In the case of multiple works in the same year, "1993a," "1993b," and so on solve the problem. (The manuals themselves will be the best resource for ascertaining the specific differences between Turabian and APA reference list formats.) The parenthetical author-date system unquestionably makes the citation process easier on the author, and that is certainly one of the main reasons that certain disciplines use it. It also enables an academic reader to know who said something, and when—on the fly, so to speak—*without* breaking rhythm to search for and internalize information pertaining to publisher, edition, editor, translator, and page numbers, all of which might not be particularly helpful in the reading process.

Parenthetical author-date citation systems do have, however, certain disadvantages:

- The parentheses chop up sentences and paragraphs, making the writing unattractive and the reading more laborious.
- This system forces the reader to read some citation material even when the reader may prefer not to, and only for the citations at the very end of the article will the citation material appear on the same page as the parenthetical interruption.
- It requires a separate bibliography, which the standard footnote or endnote system does not.
- It still requires footnotes or endnotes when ancillary material other than a citation is needed.

The protocols of the musical discipline will indicate which system is to be used, with the professor or publisher being the final arbiter.

Incomplete Citations

It often happens, particularly in older sources, that the author, publisher, or place are not identified. The standard method of dealing with this problem is to put "n.a." for "no author," "n.p." for both "no place" and "no publisher," and "n.d." for "no date." Using the same abbreviation for both place and publisher can result in the awkward-looking (n.p.: n.p., 1795), but in this case we simply have faith that the reader will be able to discern whether it is a publisher, a place, or both that a citation is lacking. A similar situation is that of "ed.," which can mean either "edition" or "edited by," and can likewise appear consecutively, with both meanings.

Finally, it is likely that you will encounter and use a bibliographic source for which you can find no format or guidelines, or which seems to blend more than one. What to do, for example, when a centuries-old source doesn't number its pages, but rather its columns of print? What about orchestral program notes for a concert you didn't attend that were later posted on a Web site? In such cases, try to follow principles gleaned from the sample citations given below (and, if you need more ideas, in Turabian and the *Chicago Manual of Style*), make logical decisions, and present all necessary information as clearly and succinctly as possible— such as, for the first example, "col. 465" or "cols. 465–66," and for the second a combination of program note and Web site citation forms. To borrow the unimprovable words of my own dissertation advisor, "try to create something as beautiful as possible."

Four reminders:

- Number all footnotes consecutively throughout a work using arabic numerals. Footnote symbols such as asterisks are no longer used.
- Footnote citations always list the author's first name first. Bibliography entries always give the last name first because bibliographies are alphabetical by author. See "Sample Citations" for examples.
- Do not number bibliography entries; simply alphabetize them. Large bibliographies may be broken down into categories such as books, journal articles, and encyclopedia entries. For smaller bibliographies, categorization is neither necessary nor desirable.

- When you are citing information contained in a footnote or endnote, include that information with the page number (e.g., 125n.6).

ABBREVIATED CITATION FORM

When you refer to a source you have already cited, it is not necessary—indeed, it is wrong—to give the full citation again. When the citations are consecutive, you need only use "Ibid." (see above, in Latin Abbreviations) and the page numbers, if different.

Fn   [32]Ibid., 38. (Or just: [32]Ibid.)

Where the citations are not consecutive, give the author's last name, an abbreviated title of the book or article, and the page number. Here are abbreviated citations that refer to citation examples 1 and 12, below:

Fn   [33]Phillip, *Early Recordings,* 36.

Fn   [34]Wegman, "Who Was Josquin?", 255.

Note: The traditional forms "op. cit." and "loc. cit." (see above, under Latin Abbreviations) have all but disappeared in abbreviated citations. "Ibid." also may be in decline, but is still an efficient and elegant designation.

SAMPLE CITATIONS

For all the following examples, citations will be given in two forms: footnote and bibliography. Since there is no doubt what the number or numbers at the end of a footnote mean, I and many others advocate omitting the use of "p." and "pp." for page and pages, as seen in the sample abbreviated notes above and citations below. Footnote citations are indicated by a superscript number that appears at the end of the sentence or phrase that contains the information cited.

Bibliography entries are different from footnotes in that the primary goal lies in providing information about a source itself, not where within that source a particular piece of information is to be found. Page numbers are only used, therefore, to locate journal and magazine articles or book chapters within the larger works in which they appear, and not at all for book-length sources. As bibliographies are arranged alphabetically, or alphabetically by section, the author's name (or, in cases of multiple authors, the first author's name) appears last name first. Other differences in format, such as use of parentheses and other matters of punctuation, will be found in the examples below.

Books by One Author

Fn [1]Robert Philip, *Early Recordings and Musical Style* (Cambridge: Cambridge University Press, 1992), 37.

B   Philip, Robert. *Early Recordings and Musical Style.* Cambridge: Cambridge University Press, 1992.

Note: Publishers' names are to be abbreviated slightly in citations by leaving out such elements as "inc." (incorporated), "and Co." (and Company), "Ltd." (Limited), or "Publishers" (*Verlag,* in German sources).

There is some disagreement over the best way to cite individual American states in cases where the publisher's city or town is not that well known. Chicago, New York, and Los Angeles need no further information; a smaller town such as Englewood Cliffs does. Using the standard two-letter postal abbreviations is an elegant solution, and results in the following citation of a publisher based in Englewood Cliffs:

Englewood Cliffs, NJ: Prentice-Hall, 2003.

Giving primacy to the best-known of like-named cities is standard practice: "Cambridge" is in England, and "Cambridge, MA" is in Massachusetts. Some believe that the postal abbreviations are too unfamiliar to non-Americans, and that (for example) "Cambridge, Mass." and "Englewood Cliffs, N.J." would be better, but I prefer the simplicity and elegance of the nonpunctuated two-letter abbreviations.

Books by Two or Three Authors

Fn [2]Homer Ulrich and Paul A. Pisk, *A History of Music and Musical Style* (New York: Harcourt, Brace, 1963), 109.

B   Ulrich, Homer, and Paul A. Pisk. *A History of Music and Musical Style.* New York: Harcourt, Brace, 1963.

Note: There is no reason to give secondary and tertiary authors' names in surname-first format, because they are not being given in alphabetical order.

Books by More Than Three Authors

Fn   ³Milo Wold and others, *An Outline History of Western Music,* 9th ed. (Boston: McGraw-Hill, 1998), 66.

B   Wold, Milo, Gary Martin, James Miller, and Edmund Cykler. *An Outline History of Western Music,* 9th ed. Boston: McGraw-Hill, 1998.

Note: For purposes of a footnote, it is sufficient to provide the name of a primary author and the page(s) within the book, but for a bibliography entry all the names—within reason, perhaps eight maximum—should be included.

Books Translated or Edited

Fn   ⁴Carl Dahlhaus, *Esthetics of Music,* trans. William W. Austin (Cambridge: Cambridge University Press, 1982), 35.

B   Dahlhaus, Carl. *Esthetics of Music.* Translated by William W. Austin. Cambridge: Cambridge University Press, 1982.

Note: Turabian/*Chicago Manual* gives different formats for acknowledging Editor and Translator; I see no reason to do so. The abbreviations "ed." and "trans." are used in footnotes but not in the bibliographic entries.

Reprints of Earlier Works

Fn   ⁵Amy Fay, *Music Study in Germany* [1908] (New York: Da Capo Press, 1979), 42.

B   Fay, Amy. *Music Study in Germany* [1908]. New York: Da Capo Press, 1979.

Note: The date given in brackets is the publication date of the edition that is being reprinted. This may not be the first edition of the work.

Book with More Than One Edition, or for Which the Translation Is More Recent, or with More Than One Editor or Translator

Fn   ⁶Jean-Jacques Eigeldinger, *Chopin: Pianist and Teacher* [1970], 3rd ed., ed. Roy Howat, trans. Naomi Shohet with Krysia Osostowicz and Roy Howat (Cambridge: Cambridge University Press, 1986), 100–102.

B   Eigeldinger, Jean-Jacques. *Chopin: Pianist and Teacher* [1970], 3rd edition. Edited by Roy Howat. Translated by Naomi Shohet with Krysia Osostowicz and Roy Howat. Cambridge: Cambridge University Press, 1986.

Note: The date of the original French edition is given in brackets so that the general age of the work, as opposed to that of the edition, may be ascertained. If there are more than three authors, editors, or translators, one can use either (e.g.) "trans. Naomi Shohet *et al.*" or "trans. Naomi Shohet and others."

Books with Additional Relevant Information Regarding Edition

Fn   ⁷Joseph Machlis and Kristine Forney, *The Enjoyment of Music* [1955], 7th ed., Chronological Version (New York: W. W. Norton, 1995), 45.

B   Machlis, Joseph and Kristine Forney. *The Enjoyment of Music* [1955], 7th edition, Chronological Version. New York: W. W. Norton, 1995.

Doctoral Dissertation

Fn   ⁸Kenneth Ross Hull, *Brahms the Allusive: Extra-Compositional Reference in the Instrumental Music of Johannes Brahms* (Ph.D. Diss., Princeton University, 1989), 37.

B   Hull, Kenneth Ross. *Brahms the Allusive: Extra-Compositional Reference in the Instrumental Music of Johannes Brahms.* Ph.D. Dissertation, Princeton University, 1989.

Note: I feel strongly that a work of the size and scope of a doctoral dissertation ought to be considered equivalent to a book rather than an article, and given italics rather than quotation marks, though that practice is common also. Note that it is important to indicate the kind of doctoral dissertation (Ph.D., D. Phil., D.M.A., D.A., etc.), and the institution and date of the degree.

Master's Thesis

Fn ⁹Conrad Edward Mary Douglas, "The Motets of Johannes Prioris, With a Prefatory Bio-Bibliographic Study" (M.M. Thesis, University of Illinois at Urbana-Champaign, 1969), 301.

B Douglas, Conrad Edward Mary. "The Motets of Johannes Prioris, With a Prefatory Bio-Bibliographic Study." M.M. Thesis, University of Illinois at Urbana-Champaign, 1974.

Note: Master's theses can be considered equivalent to published journal articles, and thus their titles are given quotation marks. As with doctoral dissertations, the species of degree, the granting institution, and the date are to be included.

Article in an Encyclopedia or Dictionary, Unsigned

Fn ¹⁰*The New Harvard Dictionary of Music,* s.v. "Nationalism."

B [In music, unsigned articles in well-known reference works are not generally listed in bibliographies, whether or not they have been cited in the footnotes.]

Note: Page numbers are unnecessary here; "s.v." stands for *sub verbo,* "under the word." When more than one edition of a reference work has appeared, the edition must be included (as with the *New Grove* article citation below).

Article in an Encyclopedia or Dictionary, Signed

Fn ¹¹Richard Orton and Hugh Davies, "Theremin," *The New Grove Dictionary of Music and Musicians,* 2nd ed., ed. Stanley Sadie (London: Macmillan, 2001), vol. 25, 387.

B Orton, Richard and Hugh Davies. "Theremin." *The New Grove Dictionary of Music and Musicians,* 2nd ed. Edited by Stanley Sadie. London: Macmillan, 2001. Vol. 25, 386–87.

Note: Precise information regarding the specific edition of any reference work, but particularly *New Grove,* as it is informally called, is necessary because articles are revised for new editions; authors are changed or added, and the articles are brought up to date. For example, this article on the theremin contains some information relating to the changing awareness of the instrument in the West after *glasnost,* which had not happened yet when the 1980 edition of the *New Grove* came out. The citations of the original article would have read this way:

Fn   ¹¹Richard Orton, "Theremin," *The New Grove Dictionary of Music and Musicians,* ed. Stanley Sadie (London: Macmillan, 1980), vol. 18, 762.

B   Orton, Richard. "Theremin." *The New Grove Dictionary of Music and Musicians.* Edited by Stanley Sadie. London: Macmillan, 1980. Vol. 18, 762–63.

Note: Whether or not a *New Grove* entry is cited in a footnote and bibliography depends on whether an author's name is provided. In almost every case, one is, and the article will need to be cited properly, but in such cases as s.v. Augmented Triad, the entry is just over a line in length and no author is given. Such cases are to be considered common knowledge, and no citation is necessary. **Important:** For citing the *New Grove Online,* see sample footnote 31.

Article or Chapter in an Anthology

Fn   ¹²Rob C. Wegman, "Who Was Josquin?", in *The Josquin Companion,* ed. Richard Sherr (Oxford and New York: Oxford University Press, 2000), 23.

B   Wegman, Rob C. "Who Was Josquin?" In *The Josquin Companion,* 21–50. Edited by Richard Sherr. Oxford and New York: Oxford University Press, 2000.

Note: When referring to an article in a larger work, the footnote identifies the page numbers of the specific information cited, whereas the bibliography gives the page numbers of the entire article. This format differs slightly from that given in Turabian (6th ed., 11.26), so as to be more consistent with the format of translated works.

Article or Chapter in a Festschrift

Fn   ¹³Albert Cohen, "Rameau on Corelli: A Lesson in Harmony," in *Convention in Eighteenth- and Nineteenth-Century Music: Essays in Honor of Leonard G. Ratner* (Stuyvesant, NY: Pendragon, 1992), 433.

B   Cohen, Albert. "Rameau on Corelli: A Lesson in Harmony." In *Convention in Eighteenth- and Nineteenth-Century Music:*

Essays in Honor of Leonard G. Ratner, 431–45. Edited by Wye J. Allanbrook, Janet M. Levy, and William P. Mahrt. Stuyvesant, NY: Pendragon, 1992.

Note: A *Festschrift* is an anthology of studies written and assembled in honor of a particular scholar, often upon his or her retirement. Whether the name of the person so honored is included in the title or not, it should be provided (in brackets if need be), since such anthologies are catalogued separately in libraries. A *Gedenkenschrift* is a similar sort of volume that memorializes a scholar after he or she is deceased.

Article in a Scholarly Journal

Fn [14] Alejandro Enrique Planchart, "The Early Career of Guillaume Du Fay," *Journal of the American Musicological Society* XLVI/3 (Fall 1993), 348.

B   Planchart, Alejandro Enrique. "The Early Career of Guillaume Du Fay." *Journal of the American Musicological Society* XLVI/3 (Fall 1993), 341–368.

Note: Some journals use roman numerals to designate volume number, and some arabic numerals; it is best to follow the journal's preference in this regard. Note that "XLVI/3," as opposed to "Vol. XLVI, no. 3," saves a good deal of space and presents the same information. Both colon and comma are in common use, and are therefore acceptable, to separate the journal volume and number and parenthetical date from the page reference. The same holds true for articles in Festschrift volumes and other anthologies.

Article in a Magazine

Fn [15]Deborah Kauffman, "The Ideas (and Words) of Friedrich Wieck," *Piano and Keyboard,* January/February 1996, 39.

B   Kauffman, Deborah. "The Ideas (and Words) of Friedrich Wieck." *Piano and Keyboard,* January/February 1996, 36–39.

Article in a Newspaper

Fn [16]Ninotchka Bennahum, "Musical Modernismo," *The Village Voice,* 1 April 1997, 83.

B   Bennahum, Ninotchka. "Musical Modernismo." *The Village Voice,* 1 April 1997, 83.

Note: Well-known newspapers, or those that include their place of origin in their names (e.g., the *Village Voice,* the *Los Angeles Times*), need not be identified geographically. In other cases, use parentheses for clarification: the *Progress-Bulletin* (Pomona, CA). When an article or news item is unsigned, simply begin the note with the title of the article or the headline appearing above it. In giving dates, "1 April 1998" is preferable to "April 1, 1998" because it does away with the comma and proceeds logically from day to month to year. That said, many publications still follow the traditional American pattern of month first, with comma.

Article or Foreword to an Edition of Music, Not by Composer

Fn   [17]Simon Rowland-Jones, preface to Joseph Haydn, *Six String Quartets Op. 33* (London: Peters, 2002), vi.

B   Rowland-Jones, Simon. Preface to Joseph Haydn, *Six String Quartets Op. 33.* London: Peters, 2002.

Note: The dates provided are those of the essay or preface and of the publication. Because publication histories of musical works tend to be very convoluted, it would be impossible to provide the same kind of information that one seeks to provide when citing other kinds of writing. When a previously written essay is published as a preface to a musical score, provide the original date of the essay in brackets, and cite the publication information of the score as above.

The pagination is important here; the musical scores begin on page 1, and whether or not pagination is provided for the front matter (title page, introductory essays, and so on) it is traditionally designated with lowercase roman numerals. When such pagination is provided, follow it; when it is not, start with the first page on which printing appears, be it the title page or something before, count up from there (i.e., i, ii, iii, iv, etc.), and put it in brackets to indicate that it was not provided.

Prefatory Notes to a Volume of the Collected Works of a Composer

Fn   [18]Karl Kroeger, Introduction to Volume III, *Complete Works of William Billings,* ed. Karl Kroeger, Hans Nathan, and Richard

Crawford (Boston: The American Musicological Society and the Colonial Society of Massachusetts, 1986), xix.

B   Kroeger, Karl. Introduction to Volume III, *Complete Works of William Billings*. Edited by Karl Kroeger, Hans Nathan, and Richard Crawford. Boston: The American Musicological Society and the Colonial Society of Massachusetts, 1986.

Article in or Preface to an Edition of Music, by Composer

Fn   [19]Colin McPhee, "Note," preface to the score of *Tabuh-Tabuhan* (New York: Associated Music Publishers, 1960), 3.

B   McPhee, Colin. "Note." Preface to the score of *Tabuh-Tabuhan*. New York: Associated Music Publishers, 1960.

Note: Where there is no title, "Preface to the score of . . ." (without the quotation marks) is sufficient.

Program Notes for a Concert

Fn   [20]Scott Warfield, program notes, North Carolina Symphony, 7–8 November 2003, 4.

B   Warfield, Scott. Program Notes. North Carolina Symphony. 7–8 November 2003.

Note: Program notes are usually not peer-reviewed, and authors can take a variety of approaches ranging from research-based scholarship to something much more casual and personal. The usual caveat lector applies.

Liner or Jacket Notes to a Sound Recording

Fn   [21]Paul Williams, notes to Procol Harum, *Shine On Brightly* (1968), LP, A & M Records SP4151.

B   Williams, Paul. Notes to Procol Harum, *Shine On Brightly*. LP, A & M Records SP4151, 1968.

Note: It is helpful to specify the kind of recording when identifying the source (see note below the following citation example for a list of formats and how they should be indicated). If there is a title to the essay, it should appear in quotation marks immediately after the author, but "notes" or something similar should still be used. Since "liner notes," "jacket notes,"

"CD notes," "CD booklet," and so on take up more space, the single word "notes" is sufficient.

DVDs, CD-ROMs, and Other Formats

Fn [22]Peter Jackson, interview on "Music of Middle-Earth," *The Lord of the Rings: Fellowship of the Ring* [2001], DVD, New Line Home Entertainment N5542 (2002).

B   "Music of Middle-Earth." *The Lord of the Rings: Fellowship of the Ring* [2001]. DVD, New Line Home Entertainment N5542, 2002.

Note: The variety of technological formats for audio and video material grows ever greater, and it is pointless to provide a format template for each when some relatively new formats are already archaic. In the case of DVD special editions of films, for example, there is no need to say which disk something appears on, but it is necessary to explain which feature (rather like an article in an anthology) something appears in, unless of course it is the feature film itself. When fashioning a citation format for an electronic source, simply provide all necessary information in a form as consistent as possible with other forms. Here is a list of formats and the way they should be indicated:

Reel Tape	Reel Tape
Cassette Tape	Cassette
Videocassette	Video
Long-Playing Record	LP
Compact Disc (audio)	CD
Laser Disc	LD
Digital Video Disc	DVD

Audio-visual materials, and the information contained in them, fit rather awkwardly into standard bibliographical reference formats. Although an album or CD release would have one release date (unless it is a reissue), for example, it is helpful to provide both the date a film was released and the date it was released on DVD. This kind of solution results in a slightly formal clumsiness, but the proper information is provided, which is the ultimate goal.

Book Review

Fn [23]Chris Goertzen, review of *Banda: Musical Life Across Borders,* by Helen Simonett, *The Journal of Musicological Research* 21/1-2 (January-May 2002), 32.

B   Goertzen, Chris. Review of *Banda: Musical Life Across Borders,*
     by Helen Simonett. *The Journal of Musicological Research*
     21/1-2 (January-May 2002), 30–33.

Recording Review

Fn   [24]Stephen D. Chakwin, Jr., review of CD recording of Haydn
     Symphonies (Collegium Musicum 90/Richard Hickox; Chandos
     0655), *American Record Guide* 63/6 (November/December
     2000), 157.

B   Chakwin, Jr., Stephen D. Review of CD recording of Haydn
     Symphonies by Collegium Musicum 90 with Richard
     Hickox, conductor, Chandos 0655. *American Record Guide*
     63/6 (November/December 2000), 157–58.

Concert Review

Fn   [25]Richard S. Ginell, "Adventures in L.A.: Berio Finishes
     Turandot, With Ambiguity," *American Record Guide* 64/5
     (September-October 2002), 21.

B   Ginell, Richard S. "Adventures in L.A.: Berio Finishes *Turandot,*
     With Ambiguity." *American Record Guide* 64/5 (September-
     October 2002), 20–22.

Note: Concert, recording, and book reviews may or may not have titles.
With concert reviews, it seems far more profitable to cite in a manner
parallel with other articles in the publication (in a journal, newspaper, or
on a Web site), rather than include the obvious term *Review* and needlessly complicate the citation. The precise format should follow the kind
of publication in which the review appears, whether journal, magazine, or
newspaper. In the case of an unsigned review, make every effort to identify the author, and if successful, give the author's name in brackets. If
not, use the following form:

> "A Good Time Was Had By All," unsigned review of a performance
> by the Cohors Luporum Ensemble, the *Courier* (Claremont, CA),
> 17 August 1974.

Personal Interview

Fn   [26]Bobby Shew, personal interview (Van Nuys, CA: 8–9 July 2002).

B   Personal interviews are not cited in bibliographies.

Note: When the interview has taken place via telephone, it is not necessary to give any geographical information.

Personal Letter

Fn   [27]Herbert L. Clarke, personal letter to Fred Elias, 30 May 1940 (author's transcript).

B   Personal letters are not cited in bibliographies.

Personal Electronic Mail Correspondence

Fn   [28]Eusebius Mandyczewski, personal email, 1 April 1998.

B   Internet posts are not cited in bibliographies.

Listserv

Fn   [29]Guido Adler, email to AMS-L (ams-1@virginia.edu; the American Musicological Society listserv), 1 April 1998.

B   Internet posts are not cited in bibliographies.

Note: Given that electronic communication, by its very nature, encourages the instantaneous response and discourages reflection and verification, email messages—particularly reactions or statements of opinion—cannot be considered as dependable as other kinds of sources. Nonetheless, in specific cases (a scholar's verification of a particular fact, for example) such communication may be used and cited. It may not be cited anonymously, regardless of whether the posting is public (i.e., to a listserv, bulletin board, or chat room) or private.

Web Site

Fn   [30]Jonathan Berger, "Brahms at the Piano,"
    http://www-ccrma.stanford.edu/ ~brg/brahms2.html (1998),
    accessed 24 April 1998.

B   Berger, Jonathan. "Brahms at the Piano."
    http://www-ccrma.stanford.edu/~brg/brahms2.html.
    1998; accessed 24 April 1998.

Note: Try to keep Web site URLs ("URL" stands for Uniform Resource Locator, the long series of characters that constitutes the address of a specific Web site) on the same line, even if an inordinate number of spaces on a previous line results. Sometimes, though, when the length of the URL exceeds the available space, this is not possible. Actual geographic location of the Web author or the server on which the Web site is maintained is irrelevant; it is only necessary to provide the information that will enable to reader to find the same data you used.

Dates for both the material cited and the day you accessed the site are necessary because people update their Web sites and the information thereon can change or disappear. Because two dates can be confusing, it is important to distinguish between them by having the date of the Web site directly follow the URL, and by explicitly using the word *accessed* for the date you visited the site. When the author provides dates for creation and revision, include both: "March 1995, rev. December 1996," enclosed within the parentheses in the footnote form and placed before the semi-colon in the bibliographic form.

FTP sites and Gopher sites are sites designed for the availability of text material only, as opposed to text and graphics (as is the case with Web sites). FTP sites make documents available for ready downloading; Gopher sites, now rare, were the precursors of modern Web sites that enabled users to navigate through menus of choices, to follow links, and so on. Citation form should follow that of Web sites because they are all sites that may be visited electronically and from which material may be downloaded. The URL will define what kind of site it is.

Online Reference Works

Fn   [31]R. Larry Todd, "Felix Mendelssohn: Oratorios and Sacred Works," *New Grove Dictionary of Music and Musicians,* 2nd ed. (online version, 2001; last updated 31 January 2002, accessed 16 April 2002), *http://www.grovemusic.com/shared/views/article. html?section=music.51795.11.*

B   Todd, R. Larry. "Felix Mendelssohn: Oratorios and Sacred Works." *New Grove Dictionary of Music and Musicians,* 2nd edition, online version, 2001. Last updated 31 January 2002, accessed 16 April 2002. *http://www.grovemusic.com/shared/ views/article.html?section=music.51795.11.*

Note: The revision/update feature available with online reference sources makes more accurate dating information available to authors, who should provide as much as they can.

Explanatory Footnotes

It is common for footnotes to contain more than citations; they might evaluate a source or engage in a bit of parenthetical commentary that is relevant to the paper but would disturb the flow of the main text. In such cases, clarity and conciseness of wording is doubly necessary.

Fn   [32]Here I follow Leonard Ratner's terminology, which defines a topic as a "subject of a musical discourse." Topics were composed of musical figures or surface characteristics that were identified with a common and well-understood dance type or musical style; see his *Classic Music* (New York: Schirmer, 1980), 9–30.

Musical Scores

There is no general agreement on the citation of musical scores. When making a specific point about a score excerpt, you should provide a musical example, either photocopied or generated on music-processing software, complete with caption, as outlined in the previous section. Scores are almost never cited in footnotes; an in-text reference accompanied by the score example is sufficient.

Whether or not to include scores in bibliographies is a decision to be made by your professor or publisher. Musical scores are not often included in published bibliographies, but many professors want citations of all the resources a student author has used. Source studies, in which a variety of different editions (and, perhaps, manuscripts and sketches) are compared, require bibliographic citation of scores. The following formats may be used:

B   Hovhaness, Alan. *Bacchanale.* New York: Peters, [c1968].
B   Chavez, Carlos. *Sinfonia de Antigona* (1933). Manuscript score. Department of Special Collections, Green Library, Stanford University, Stanford, CA.
B   Holiday, David. *Four Dances for Twenty-Five Dollars* (1985). Composer's Score.

Note: Published music often omits the date of publication, in which case it is acceptable to rely on the informed conjecture of the individual who produced the library's citation record. Simply putting "score" is unnecessary, but indicating manuscript, or composer's personal copy, or another such designation can be helpful.

LAST-MINUTE CORRECTIONS

Given even the best intentions, the most industrious work habits, and the very latest technology, you may still find minor typographical errors in your submission draft, errors that you want to correct but for which you cannot justify using the paper for an additional printing. You may correct these typos in pen, delicately and neatly. Traditional manuscript editing symbols, which are as appropriate to such circumstances as they are for editing and correcting student papers, include:

beethoven the Composer	Capitalize; change to lower case
pianomusic	Insert a space
pinao	Reverse letters (or words)
piano	Delete
pi ano	Close up space
¶	Begin a new paragraph here

Index

A Writer's Checklist

1. Have I correctly understood the assignment?

2. Do I have something to say, and have I said it clearly and concisely, avoiding needlessly inflated language?

3. Have I used transitions between sentences and paragraphs so that readers will be guided smoothly through my thought process?

4. Has this paper been through at least three drafts, each subject to a thorough editing and proofreading?

5. Have I read this paper aloud at least twice, making improvements in the writing in the places where I stumbled or found awkward wording?

6. Has the scholarly apparatus (footnotes, musical examples, example captions, etc.) been completely verified and correctly formatted?

7. Have I preserved all my notes, drafts, and databases for future reference?

8. Have I made a photocopy of this assignment for my own records?

9. Is there a title page with appropriate information?

10. Have the pages been clipped, stapled, or bound?